KNOX

the Anatomist

For a hundred years English surgeons have remained complacent at the obloquy exclusively heaped on the head of the unfortunate Dr Knox in connection with the Burke and Hare murders. . . . Knox was hounded out of society to wander up and down the country for years as a sort of surgeons' scapegoat.

CECIL HOWARD TURNER
The Inhumanists (1932)

Robert Knox. An engraving from a calotype taken of Dr Knox in his fiftieth year.

From *A Sketch of the Life and Writings of Robert Knox* by Henry Lonsdale (Macmillan & Co., 1870).

KNOX

the Anatomist

ISOBEL RAE

OLIVER & BOYD

EDINBURGH & LONDON

1964

OLIVER AND BOYD LTD

Tweeddale Court
Edinburgh 1

39A Welbeck Street
London, W.1

First published 1964

Printed in Great Britain by
Oliver and Boyd Ltd, Edinburgh

ACKNOWLEDGMENTS

I AM indebted to the Royal College of Surgeons of Edinburgh for permission to quote from their records, and from C. H. Creswell's History of the College, *Royal College of Surgeons of Edinburgh*.

I am also grateful to James A. Ross, F.R.C.S.ED., and Hugh W. Y. Taylor for allowing me to quote from their article "Robert Knox's Catalogue," *Journal of the History of Medicine and Allied Sciences*, x. No. 3 (1955); to Messrs Oliver & Boyd Ltd for permission to quote from James Moores Ball, *The Sack-'em-up Men*; to Mrs Frieda Sandwith for permission to quote from her book *Surgeon Compassionate*; and to the Royal Society of Edinburgh and the Royal Marsden Hospital, London, for information about Dr Knox.

I. R.

ILLUSTRATIONS

IN the month of December of the year 1828, the usually staid and sober city of Edinburgh went wild with excitement. On 2 November, the discovery and identification of a woman's body in the cellar of Dr Knox's anatomical school had revealed the nefarious practices of the murderers Burke and Hare. Soon it was known that at least fifteen other persons had been similarly done to death, and rumour magnified the numbers. All sorts of stories began to fly around the town, broadsides were published to acquaint the public with all the lurid details, and during the week before Burke's trial, which was fixed for Christmas Eve, no less than 8,000 extra copies of the Edinburgh newspapers were printed between Thursday morning and Saturday night in order to satisfy the curiosity of the citizens.

The public imagination had been deeply stirred by this new and terrible crime, because all the victims had been murdered solely for the money which their dead bodies would fetch as anatomical material.

By chance Burke and Hare had taken the bodies not to the University School of Anatomy, but to that of an extra-mural lecturer, Dr Robert Knox; and henceforward his name was to be inseparably linked with theirs. People were in no mood to differentiate between the degrees of culpability of those involved in the scandal; it was enough that Dr Knox had bought the bodies. Public opinion held him to be as guilty of murder as Burke and Hare, who had smothered their victims without remorse.

Even informed opinion tended to take this line, with the result that Dr Knox has rarely been considered apart from Burke and Hare. It is true that one of his students, Dr Henry Lonsdale, tried to remedy this situation by writing his biography in 1870, but it is a rather heavy Victorian tome and it reached only a small public. In our own times, James Bridie wrote a play, *The Anatomist*, which was produced in Edinburgh in 1930, but as a dramatist, he naturally concentrated on the events of the year

1828, when he could show the murderers going about their business. Dr Knox appears fleetingly in this play, but neither Bridie nor Dylan Thomas in his film script *The Doctor and the Devils* has produced a living likeness of this brilliant anatomist who, when he was still under forty, had his life's work ruined by the Burke and Hare scandal, yet fought on undaunted for another thirty-three years, until he died in 1862.

Now, so near to the centenary of his death, the moment seems fitting for some reassessment of his character and a restatement of his story.

Robert Knox was an Edinburgh man. He was born in that city on 4 Sep. 1793,[1] the eighth child and fifth son of Robert and Mary Knox, who were both of farming stock, but—and it may have some bearing on his hereditary characteristics—whereas his father came of a line of Kirkcudbright tenant farmers, who claimed kinship with John Knox, the Reformer, his mother (Mary Sherer or Schrerer) was of German extraction.

To be born in Edinburgh towards the end of the eighteenth century was indeed to be born in a happy hour. Intellectually Edinburgh was then enjoying a "golden Age," and although by the last decade of the century, some of her more eminent sons, such as David Hume, Adam Smith, and Allan Ramsay, were already dead, they had left a precious heritage behind them and had advanced Scotland to the van of European thought. At this time, too, the fame of Edinburgh University and its Medical School was widespread, both in England and on the Continent.

Edinburgh was by no means immune from the new and revolutionary ideas which issued from France in the years after 1789. For example, until Henry Dundas suppressed them, there were in existence several clubs connected directly or indirectly with the "Friends of the People" Society, and to one of these Robert Knox, senior, was said to belong. It was also said that he had made his peace with Dundas at the expense of his former friends in the movement; at any rate, he showed no desire to become a martyr and follow the convicted Palmer and Muir to

[1] The date is sometimes given as 1791; but Knox's death certificate gives his age as sixty-nine in 1862.

2

Botany Bay, which was just as well for his family. He was by profession a school-master, a teacher of Natural Philosophy, and Mathematics master at George Heriot's School. He was therefore well qualified to give his son Robert the elements of his education at home; this he did because, for a time, the boy was in rather poor health after an attack of small-pox.

The Jesuits claim that if they can have a child to train for the first six years of his life, then the pattern is determined for the future, whatever manner of education he may later receive. This theory would seem to be true in the case of young Robert Knox; the stamp was set by his father, and the imprint deepened by his schooling, so that in order to understand the mature man it is necessary to know something of his early years. Although his father was not prepared to suffer unduly for his principles, he must have sown in his son's mind that love of France and French thought which in his middle years became almost an obsession. Young Robert must also have absorbed revolutionary views from his father, and "liberal opinions" from Dr Alexander Adam, the Rector of the Edinburgh High School, which he attended from the age of twelve.

Dr Adam was one of the High School's most famous head-masters, and the School, the Scholia Regia Edinensis of King James VI, had been founded as a Grammar School in the sixteenth century. He could count Sir Walter Scott, John and Charles Bell, and Lord Brougham among his pupils—the latter said of him that "he had the talent of making his pupils delight in learning," even if he did express those liberal opinions of his "somewhat unguardedly." But Dr Adam was first and foremost a classical scholar, and he laid great emphasis on the teaching of Latin. Writing, arithmetic, and geography also formed an important part of the curriculum, but it is interesting to note how much of the intellectual training was achieved through the medium of the Latin tongue, rarely can a scientist have had such a thorough classical grounding as had the anatomist, Robert Knox.

The system of education at the Edinburgh High School was very unlike that of an English public school, and Knox early learned the value of hard work with little intermission. The

3

six hundred boys were given very few holidays; six weeks in the autumn, otherwise only on "sacramental occasions," as Dr Adam considered that "boys were surely much the worse for long vacations." In winter there were no "play days" in the afternoon except on Saturday, and in summer only on Wednesday and Saturday and then only for "such boys as have been attentive through the week." The sports appear to have been shinty, football, "clacken" (a sort of fives), leaping, wrestling, and running; whether Knox excelled in any of them has not been recorded.

Instruction was given by the Rector and four classical masters. Each of them received a class of beginners quadrennially, and these, until they reached their fifth year and the Rector's class, proceeded up the School under the direction of that same master, and the classes never mixed. This being so, the class in which a new boy happened to find himself was a matter of some moment to him. Robert Knox was fortunate in being placed in that of Mr James Gray, M.A., who has been described by another teacher as having "something like the inspiration of genius in everything he said and did, he was an exceedingly warm-hearted, benevolent and enthusiastic man." He was also an excellent Greek scholar, and a former Rector of the Grammar School of Dumfries, where he had taught the sons of Robert Burns, and been on friendly terms with the poet.

His new pupil, Robert Knox, was to become one of the great teachers and lecturers of his day, and Knox certainly, although perhaps unconsciously, acquired some of his technique from his masters. Mr Gray taught by a system of question and answer, the questions being put "with great rapidity, force and precision, and answered in the same style." The Rector's method was to walk up and down as he taught, never sitting at his desk, and his "attitudes and motions were very animated"; in one hand he held a book or his spectacles, in the other his tawse, which as he was no believer in corporal punishment, he flourished but rarely used.

There was considerable competition to get into the Rector's fifth-year class, and such was its fame that several of its hundred boys came from other schools and other countries. Dr Adam controlled them all without difficulty, and gave the final polish to their classical education. They studied Caesar, Livy, Sallust, Virgil, Horace, and Terence, and every Friday they wrote a Latin exercise from English prose dictated by the Rector; exercises—translations from the Latin author they were studying —had to be done at home, and translations from Virgil into English verse were encouraged but not compulsory. Dr Adam expected a thorough knowledge of his own *Grammar* and *Roman Antiquities*.

Knox had just begun his last year in this class when, in December 1809, Dr Adam died. He was succeeded by Mr Pillans, another gifted classical scholar, and Knox remained at the High School under him until the end of the school year. Then, in August 1810, he left as Dux and Gold Medallist, no small achievement, and was the recipient of a prize, a folio edition of Virgil, given by the Lord Provost and Town Council of Edinburgh, the patrons of the School.

In spite of this the name of Robert Knox occurs in none of those lists of eminent pupils in the High School histories. Proud as the authorities were to claim as former pupils such men as Lord Jeffrey, Lord Brougham, Dugald Stewart, and Sir Walter Scott, they seem to have adopted the "correct" Edinburgh attitude towards Dr Knox, and probably would have expunged his name, had that been possible, from their records. It is useless to look in their archives for any anecdotes of the anatomist's school days.

In November 1810, three months after leaving the High School, Robert Knox enrolled as a medical student at the University of Edinburgh. He did not, as was very usual in those days, take the Arts course first, perhaps because he was seventeen and older than the majority of his fellow students, perhaps because of the adequacy of the High School education, or perhaps just because he wished to concentrate immediately on medicine. Although the M.D. diploma of the University of Edinburgh was notoriously difficult to obtain and many candidates failed at their first attempt, it should have offered no great obstacle to anyone with Robert Knox's scholastic record and yet, when the future anatomist stood for examination at the end of the three years' course, he failed—and failed in Anatomy. It was to take him a fourth year to win the coveted degree, but his ultimate success was "more startling than his previous rejection."

It may not have been entirely his fault that he failed in that first Anatomy examination. Practical Anatomy was not then actively encouraged in the Medical School; "a haphazard sort of study"[2] Knox himself called it, for dissection was not an examination subject and most students were satisfied with what they could learn from the pages and illustrations of books. Nor was the Professor of Anatomy, Alexander Monro, *tertius*, an inspiration to his class. By 1813 the three generations of Monros—*primus*, *secundus*, and *tertius*, grandfather, father, and son—had, between them, held the Chair of Anatomy for over eighty years and the light of genius was beginning to burn low. Not that Alexander Monro, *tertius*, was not an able man; he did in fact give a "clear, precise, complete course of lectures," but he was insufferably bored by the whole business. One of his students refers to his "unimpassioned indifference" as a lecturer, and this must surely be an understatement as another report describes how he would read his grandfather's lectures to his own classes without taking the trouble to alter the dates, and even the shower of peas which greeted his statement that he had been a student in Leyden in 1719 failed to rouse him.

From about 1804 onwards, serious medical students and canny Scots at that, "even after they had paid their fee to Monro," deserted him to attend the lectures of his extra-mural rival, Dr John Barclay, and it was to him that Robert Knox turned in his hour of need in 1813. Barclay was the absolute antithesis of Monro: "as a lecturer he was all fire and zeal, and intent that his students should learn." His lectures were lightened by historical interludes, little strokes of humour, and sometimes a witty anecdote. Barclay had originally been educated for the Church, but afterwards discovered his true vocation and studied medicine at Edinburgh and London, returning to Edinburgh to become assistant to John Bell, founder of the subject of Surgical Anatomy, who until 1799 owned a most successful anatomical school in the city. Very soon Barclay left Bell in order to work independently, and he quickly attracted a class of about 300 students, a class so

[2] *Lancet*, 11 Nov. 1854.

large that it had to be divided into two groups, to which he lectured at 11 a.m. and 6 p.m. Knox had found a master after his own heart, for Barclay was a dedicated man. To his students he proclaimed:

> "Anatomy is an art, and those who would study it must see it practised: they must see the forms, magnitudes, positions, proportions, and connections of the structures and organs as they are in nature. No figures or verbal descriptions can ever compensate for want of the originals; they give not the same relish nor interest, nor afford the same correctness of ideas. . . . The information which enters by the eye and is proved by the touch is very different from that which enters merely by the ear."

Barclay gave his class demonstrations from dissections, followed by surgical operations, and spent all day in his class-room and dissecting-room, where he was always accessible to his students, being the first teacher of Anatomy habitually to work with them. By the end of the year there was no fear that young Knox would fail a second time in Anatomy. What was even more important was that he had found inspiration for his life's work: he would be an anatomist, and for Knox the definition of an anatomist was "a man gifted with the desire to know the unknown."[3]

When the time for the examination came round again, Knox was not only well prepared but he still had at his command from his High School education "the choicest Latin," which was fortunate, as the whole examination was conducted in that tongue. It was a terrifying ordeal which has been graphically described by Sir Robert Christison who endured it about this time, when "the custom was for the Medical Faculty to meet for examination successively at one another's houses, and for the host to bear the chief brunt of duty." Christison attended in the evening, as we may presume Knox did, in evening dress, and sat at a table round which all the medical professors were assembled, each in turn questioning him. By Dr Gregory, Professor of the Practice of Physic (the inventor of Gregory's Powder), he was examined for an hour on the anatomy, physiology, and diseases of the stomach, with their treatment, and the chemistry of some of the remedies mentioned. The other five professors then proceeded to put further questions, but luckily not at such length. As well as the

[3] *Great Artists and Great Anatomists*, London 1852, p. 10.

oral examination the candidate had to answer written questions on the aphorisms of Hippocrates, and give an opinion on a case-history presented to him, and then, after giving proof that he had attended classes in Anatomy and Surgery, Chemistry, Botany, Materia Medica and Pharmacy, the Theory and Practice of Medicine, and the lectures in Clinical Medicine given in the Royal Infirmary, he had to write a thesis in Latin, have it printed at his own expense, and defend it on Graduation Day.

In 1814 Robert Knox accomplished all this successfully. In fact the thesis which he wrote on "De Viribus Stimulantium et Narcoticorum in corpore sano" reached a standard higher than that usually attained in these theses, and was commended by his professors. In it he recorded the effects of alcohol and other stimulants and narcotics upon the human body, and also the effect of exercise upon the pulse, a subject which he expanded in January of the following year in an article published in the *Edinburgh Medical and Surgical Journal*, and later in a paper read to the Royal Society of Edinburgh. His most interesting conclusions were that early rising might be conducive to long life and that alcohol was definitely detrimental:

> These [spirituous] liquors in my opinion are purely medicinal. Their daily or even frequent use in any climate or in any quantity, I apprehend to be a great error in regimen, and can never be required. I think them directly opposed to the enjoyment of perfect health and strength.

He acted on these findings; throughout his life he rose early, and drank little in a far from abstemious society.

After obtaining his degree Dr Knox went for a short holiday to the Highlands, and then in the autumn, like so many of his contemporaries, he set out for London to finish his education by becoming a pupil of the famous surgeon, John Abernethy, at St. Bartholomew's Hospital. Knox was certainly no self-taught genius: he had learned much from his High School masters and from John Barclay, and now he was to learn more from a man whom the historian of his hospital called "the greatest teacher, the most lucid expositor, the most eloquent lecturer of his time."

By 1814, John Abernethy had been giving anatomical and

surgical lectures for twenty-six years, and so successful had he been that, in 1791, the Governors of St. Bartholomew's Hospital built a new lecture-theatre to house the hundreds of students attracted by his fame. It was to this building, later pulled down, and very overcrowded in his day, that the young Knox came.

Knox had gone to Abernethy for what he could teach him of Surgery and Physiology: there was little he could learn from him about Practical Anatomy as Abernethy affected to despise it, and even went so far as to tell his students: "I can't teach you anatomy—you must learn it for yourselves." Knox attributed this attitude to "natural indolence and the spirit of his age and country,"[4] and regretted the manner in which the great man

> talked of the abdominal muscles as so many steaks which he, buffoon-like, tossed over each other, when dissected, counting them as steak first, steak second, steak third, muscles and tendons which the first of descriptive anatomists have failed clearly to describe.

Dr Knox certainly did not adopt Abernethy's mannerisms, which tended to give the impression of a somewhat eccentric and uncouth personality, but he may well have modelled his style of lecturing on his master's. Abernethy never forgot the difficulties of his task; he would "unravel" a complicated subject as if he were a student coming to it for the first time, and he would enliven his lecture with apposite anecdotes, so that he never lost the attention of his class. Even the most careless student remembered what Abernethy had taught him, and to Knox, who was far from careless, it was immensely stimulating to listen to the great surgeon's exposition of his art, that of "a man of high genius," as Knox said.

Fortunately Knox was able to finish the 1814-15 session at St. Bartholomew's under Abernethy, although in the new year the war clouds were again gathering over Europe. On 15 February 1815 Napoleon Bonaparte made his escape from Elba; on 16 June Robert Knox was gazetted Hospital Assistant to the Forces, and a few days later, after the battle of Waterloo on 18 June, he was sent to Brussels to attend the wounded.

[4] *Lancet*, 11 Nov. 1854.

9

Free from the shackles of student life, Robert Knox, who was always something of a dandy, must have been quite pleased to see himself in his military uniform, with the plumed hat and long sword habitually worn by army surgeons. Knox always had a soldierly bearing, and, although not very tall, was a powerfully built, broad-shouldered man. But Fate had not been altogether kind to him, as the attack of small-pox from which he suffered in childhood had sadly ravaged the left side of his face. His left eye had atrophied, leaving only the socket, and the disease had also coarsened his features and lined his cheeks, so that his students gave him the nickname of "Old Cyclops." Although Dr Knox was "the plainest visaged man in Edinburgh" he had great charm, and of both these facts he was well aware.

But charm and fine uniforms had passed from Brussels with the Duchess of Richmond's ball. When Knox arrived in the city the uniforms were caked in mud and blood, and the doctors were working night and day, "with scarcely an interval for refreshment and none for repose." The losses at Waterloo had been, as Wellington said, "immense"—over 7,000 wounded—and Brussels was totally unprepared for the reception of casualties on this scale. The citizens did their best, but it was inevitable in the circumstances that it could be no more than a makeshift. Professor John Thomson described how:

> On the day after the battle . . . the shops were shut, the people were at their doors administering cordials, and offering dressing to the wounded, taking the tenderest care of them. . . . Hundreds of wounded were to be seen in the streets, and some were to be found in every home. Even after the hospitals were fully established, several hundreds of privates, beside the officers, were voluntarily received and taken care of by the inhabitants during their cure.

Notwithstanding all this, many of the soldiers had to wait for days to have their wounds dressed, and there were many piteous scenes. Sir Charles Bell, the famous surgeon and younger brother of John Bell, left London for Brussels as soon as he heard news of the battle, and even he, who had made a special study of the gun-shot wounds of the Peninsular War, confessed that he came dangerously near to being "out-manned" by the sights he saw at Brussels. He had offered to do all the capital operations and for almost a week he operated daily, until his clothes were stiff with blood and his arms "powerless with the exertion of using the knife." As he had volunteered to operate on the French wounded, because he thought they had the worst gun-shot wounds, he performed many of these operations under the eye of Hospital-Assistant Knox, and all, of course, were done without anaesthetics and without antiseptics. Knox, in charge of the wards of the 1st Division, had been posted to the hospital where the French prisoners were lying: they were in a very bad state, as many of them had been in hiding for several days and were suffering from fever and lack of food as well as from their untended wounds.[5] The hospital itself was far from ideal as it was situated in the lowest and most unhealthy part of the city, in a building formerly occupied as a barrack by the *Gens-d'armerie*. Although Professor John Thomson (who had gone to Brussels from Edinburgh) spoke well of the cleanliness of the hospitals: "the beds, in general, excellent and the supply of bed-clothes such as to allow of their being changed as often as necessary," Knox mentioned the small and stuffy rooms of the *gendarmerie* hospital, and attributed to them the outbreak of hospital gangrene which proved so fatal to his patients.

In after years Knox would speak of the valuable experience he gained at Brussels, but he also told his friend and biographer, Lonsdale, that only one of Sir Charles Bell's secondary amputations survived, and that the people of Brussels did not think very much of the English Medical Department. Certainly, some of the Army surgeons at this time—before Sir James McGrigor's reforms—were deplorably ignorant and lacking in skill. The sights which Dr Knox saw so early in his career clearly impressed upon him the absolute necessity of sound anatomical training for safe surgery. He was shocked and distressed by his experiences, and considered that it would have been preferable to tend the wounded in the open field, "so terrible to behold"[6] was the mortality in general hospitals.

[5] *Lancet*, 17 May 1856.
[6] *Ibid.*

B   11

After three weeks, when his patients were convalescent, Dr Knox was sent home in charge of a party of ninety wounded, the first to return to England. He had to escort them from Ostend to Haslar Hospital, and he described how, as soon as he reached the deck of the cross-Channel boat, he realised that he would have to put John Abernethy's precepts into practice:

> A young Englishman lay extended on the deck, pale, exhausted, almost exsanguineous, and seemingly dying. He spoke with difficulty. The wound below the ear had never closed, and it bled daily, so that he could no longer sit upright. As usual a pile of rags, lint, portions of bandages, etc., steeped in blood and now hardened, concealed the wound, and kept the danger out of sight. The sergeant, my only assistant, cautioned me not to remove this pile, as he had seen the dangerous results repeatedly in this case. Regardless of this, I put Mr Abernethy's plan in force: removed all pressure, exposed the wound to the air, applied a rag loosely to the wound, directing it to be constantly wetted with vinegar, and directed his head to be raised on pillows. The haemorrhage never returned, and he rapidly recovered.[7]

From Haslar Dr Knox was sent to take charge "with others" of Melsea Hospital in Hampshire, an emergency hospital established to relieve the garrison hospitals of Portsmouth, Portsea, and Gosport.[8] Very little is known of Knox's spell of duty at Melsea, and after about a year he was gazetted to the 72nd Regiment (later the Seaforth Highlanders); with this Regiment in 1817, he set sail for the Cape of Good Hope. In those days the voyage from England, under sail, took about two months, and with the enthusiasm of scientific youth, Knox decided not to waste a minute of the weeks he had to spend on board. He brought out his thermometers and three times daily, at 6 a.m., noon, and 6 p.m., he took the temperature of the "North Atlantic Ocean and the Superincumbent Atmosphere" and later published his findings in the *Edinburgh Philosophical Journal*. He also dissected sharks and dolphins, and wrote a paper on his observations "On the Action of the Heart in Fishes,"[9] and propounded a theory that some fish possess a sixth sense [10] (between touch and hearing)

[7] *Lancet*, 17 May 1856.
[8] *Medical Times*, 28 Jun. 1851.
[9] *Edinburgh Medical and Surgical Journal*, xviii. 564.
[10] *Brewster's Journal of Science*, ii. 12.

so that "the undulation of the water by a tolerably sized ship might affect these organs at a distance, and thus apprize the shark of the presence of a moving body." That he was a good sailor is manifest in his description of the tropical storms encountered in November; he was young enough to enjoy the excitement of the lashing rain, the furling of the sails, the straining of the masts, as the ship battled her way against the gale. Taking it all in all, Hospital-Assistant Knox may have been quite sorry when at last he came within sight of Table Mountain.

In Cape Town, as a young officer fresh from England, he was well received; he moved, he tells us, in the "first society," so presumably he had the entrée to Government House, with all its parties and balls. The Governor in 1817 was Lord Charles Somerset (second son of the 5th Duke of Beaufort, and brother of Lord Fitzroy Somerset, later Lord Raglan) who had only been in office for three years, and found the conditions in the Colony most disturbing. He had every reason to be disturbed, as the situation on the Great Fish River, the so-called frontier between the white settlers and the natives, made it impossible to guarantee security of tenure to the Dutch farmers along the river banks, who were constantly being harried by Bantu raiders.

Lord Charles, soon after his arrival, had made a tour of the province and had reported to London that "the terror is general in the Zuurveld" (later known as the Albany district). He begged for a supply of English emigrants who could be settled on the frontier where the white population was obviously too sparse to offer any resistance to the invaders. Lord Charles got his settlers, but not until 1820. Meanwhile it was in the midst of these constantly deteriorating conditions that Knox found himself on his arrival at the Cape.

It was strange that he should have been sent there at all, because, at that time, the Government at home, for reasons of economy, was reducing the Cape garrisons below the minimum of safety; by October 1817 the troops numbered only 2,744. Knox, one fears, must have been part of what one historian calls "the useless reinforcements which arrived about the time the others left." What was even worse was that the dregs of the Army appear to have been sent to South Africa; some of the men were criminals

13

and many were captured deserters who, when they arrived, were drafted to the 1st Battalion of the 60th Regiment, with the result that at one point the 72nd Regiment to which Knox was attached had to be employed to protect the people of Simonstown not only from their frontier foes, but also from the men of the 60th Regiment. It was no wonder that the Kaffirs took heart and began their depredations again; many head of cattle were stolen, and a weak Commando expedition, sent to recapture them, did more harm than good by inviting reprisals.

It was fortunate that after a year in South Africa Dr Knox was in good training. He had not devoted too much time to the pleasures of Cape Town; for he had become one of the crack shots of the Regiment and "tireless in the saddle," he would ride for ninety miles "without the slightest fatigue" on his fine Arab mare. Both accomplishments were soon to be put to the test. By the end of December 1818, there were 18,000 Kaffirs drawn up ready to cross the Fish River; and by the end of January 1819, they had infiltrated deeply into the district of Albany, stealing hundreds of cattle, and brutally murdering officers and men on the frontier patrol. A really powerful force now had to be brought against the raiders, and by calling out mounted burghers from the towns and gathering together what infantry regiments there were, including the 72nd Regiment, the Government collected a grand total of 3,352 men, not a moment too soon, as on 22 April 1819 the Kaffirs attacked Grahamstown itself.

Although the Kaffirs heavily outnumbered the defenders, their assegais were no match for muskets, and they were repulsed, leaving 1,000 dead behind them. A punitive expedition was then organised, under Colonel Willshire, to pursue them into Kaffirland. The left wing of this body was made up of the Dutch mounted burghers under their own leader, Andries Stockenstrom, Landdrost of Graaf Reinet, and he recorded that the only other military man with him in the force was Dr Robert Knox,

> who, by his great abilities, not only in his medical capacity, but as a man of general knowledge and science, rendered great service, especially in tracing the nature of horse distemper, by the dissection of the many

subjects which unfortunately daily presented themselves, and his enlightened political and ethnological views were deeply interesting to me during the many months he remained under my command.

Their task was arduous as they had been ordered to scour the Fish River jungles where the Kaffirs were hiding, and this meant marching by night and day, "creeping into the narrowest footpaths, and descending the steepest precipices."

That, presumably, was the time when the incident occurred which later formed the subject of one of Dr Knox's best after-dinner stories, told to illustrate how "the anatomical knowledge of a Kaffir proved fatal to a band of British soldiers." These men had to cross a wooded ravine in single file, and when they gave no signal of having reached the bottom, their Captain grew anxious and sent a second party down by another route. They found their companions lying dead in their own blood; as each man had stepped down, a Kaffir had plunged his knife into the artery in his neck, "and so expert was he in stabbing the vital part, that the Britisher fell at once, and never uttered a groan."

Despite unpleasant incidents such as this, Stockenstrom successfully carried out the mopping-up operations and rejoined the main force, and by the autumn of 1819 the Kaffirs had to admit defeat. On 15 October 1819 Lord Charles Somerset came from Cape Town to interview the chiefs and arrange an amicable settlement, which he succeeded in doing, even though the Kaffirs' frontier was moved still further east from the Great Fish River to the Keiskamma and the intervening territory was declared neutral. In this wild and beautiful country two forts were ordered to be built, and to expedite the building, all the regular forces—including the 72nd Regiment and Hospital-Assistant Knox—were encamped alongside, ready to act as builders or as guards. More often as builders, since the New Year of 1820 brought peace at last to the frontier.

This then was the sequence of events in the Kaffir War in which Knox served; so, while his service included short spells of hard fighting interspersed with long periods of leisure, it was not for Knox synonymous with boredom, for afterwards he would often refer to his happy days "on the slopes and tangled rocky dells of the Anatola."

During hostilities Knox had, as Stockenstrom reported, taken every chance that offered "of dissecting the many subjects which unfortunately daily presented themselves," but there is no truth whatever in the libellous statement, made after the Burke and Hare affair, that he had "walked out of his tent and shot as many Kaffirs as he wanted for scientific and ethnological purposes." Knox was, on the whole, pro-Kaffir, he always extolled the tribesmen for their courageous conduct, and was apt not to condone his countrymen's part in the war against them. Although Edinburgh was later shocked by his remarks on the subject, it must be remembered that Knox had been on the spot and knew what he was talking about, and that there were two sides to the question. It could be argued, and was in fact so argued (Committee on Aborigines 1836) that we, the British,

> interfered with the quarrel between Paramount Chief Gaika and other Kaffir tribes . . . so that, in the first instance, in consequence of our interference, we obtained a considerable quantity of the personal property of these natives; and in the second place, we obtained a considerable space of territory.

Already, in 1820, Robert Knox held sufficiently advanced opinions to make him a supporter of equality and fraternity—an early and unfashionable anti-colonialist.

Such liberal views might make him popular with Landdrost Stockenstrom, but as he was to discover when he returned home, to express them in Edinburgh was the surest way to antagonise the great majority of his fellow countrymen. The Rev. Sydney Smith had no illusions about this when he wrote some years later:

> From the beginning of the century to the death of Lord Liverpool [11] was an awful period for those who ventured to maintain liberal opinions . . . Jacobin, leveller, atheist, Socinian, incendiary, regicide, were the gentlest appellations used; and any man who breathed a syllable against the senseless bigotry of the two Georges or hinted at the abominable tyranny and persecution exercised against Catholic Ireland, was shunned as unfit for the relations of social life. Not a murmur against any abuse was permitted.

When the war was over Knox turned his attention to the South African fauna. At one time he employed quite a staff of

[11] Lord Liverpool was Prime Minister from 1812-27.

men to skin the beasts he had shot or trapped, and to help him with the preparation of the skeletons, on which he made notes which were of the utmost value to him in later years. Knox always spoke with horror of the pain inflicted on animals by unnecessary vivisection, so he took no pleasure in this hunting and killing. He never engaged in blood sports, and said, "I never viewed as a sport the destruction of any animal."[12] Nearly twenty years later he wrote:

> I have, all my life, had a natural horror for experiments made on living animals, nor has more matured reason altered my feelings with regard to these vivisections, but rather confirmed me in the belief that for the most part they are wholly unnecessary, and therefore highly to be reprobated. A minute and careful anatomy, aided by observation of the numerous experiments made by nature and accident on man himself, seems to me to present infinitely the best and surest basis for physiological and pathological science.[13]

That he was a great animal lover is shown by the well-known story of his professional treatment of a lion in the Edinburgh Zoo where, fixing a lancet to the end of a long stick, he punctured an abscess on the animal's swollen fore-paw, to its great relief.

Knox was one of the earliest of the African explorers, and like other explorers after him, he had good stories to tell of his experiences and told them probably rather better than most. To the learned societies of Edinburgh he spoke on his return of the wild creatures of the Cape; of the hyena, a "solitary beast" that he had often tracked to its den, and of the serpents and poisonous snakes that he had encountered.

Yet, had Knox so desired, he might never have returned to Edinburgh. Living as he did on the frontier of Kaffirland, he realised how important it was for everyone concerned that there should be a proper line of demarcation, and to this end he set himself to correct and extend the charts of the Cape territory. For this work he received the official thanks of the Army Medical Department from the Director-General himself, Sir James McGrigor, who commended his "industry, zeal and talents." Indeed Dr Knox's interest in the frontier district was so great that

---

[12] *Fish and Fishing in the Lone Glens of Scotland*, London and New York 1854.
[13] *Lancet*, 1838-9. II.

he helped to plan an important road to open up the interior of the country, and did so with such success that he was offered the post of surveyor to a part of the colony. Simultaneously the Dutch settlers invited him to be chief surgeon to the Dutch Free States, as he had become a great favourite with the Dutch burgher commando troops with whom he had served in the war.

Assuredly the ball was at his feet, and yet Knox, after little more than a year at the Cape, was thinking of his future only in terms of his return to Scotland. Perhaps he knew that, for all his many and varied successes in the Colony, South Africa was for him no more than a blind-alley. Perhaps also he was homesick; for, although he had four elder brothers, he was looked upon— after the early death of his father in 1812—as the head of his family, and he took full responsibility for the care of his mother, to whom he was devoted. On 10 September 1818 he wrote to his youngest brother, Fred:

My dearest Brother,

By your letters, I perceive that neither time nor absence has in the smallest degree diminished the affections of my relations, or attachment of my friends. How happy am I, and yet how wretched! Delighted to hear of your health and prosperity, yet miserable at the thoughts of the wide-extended ocean which rolls between us.

I am in tolerable health, and as far as regards all the comforts of life every way content. You know, and to you I may say it without vanity, I generally acquire friends wherever I go, and the Cape forms no exception to this remark; indeed I know nothing but the first society. . . . My banishment cannot last for ever, and I have already taken such steps as will probably allow of my returning before June 1819. I begin, my dear brother, to "lack promotion": life is short, and excessive studies have not a little impaired my constitution. It is true that in this country I could settle advantageously for life, nay, perhaps acquire a fortune in ten or fifteen years, but will this recompense me for so long a deprivation of European society?—the separation from all those whom I hold most dear, from friends, from relations, from my beloved parent? All the wealth of India could never reconcile me to this. Home I must and shall, life permitting, once more behold.

I have been necessitated to resign the pen for the gun, to acquire the art of managing the reins of my horse whilst travelling on the parched roads of Africa, or pursuing at full speed the swift antelope over the pathless flats whose termination the weariest eye searches for in vain. The amusements of the chase, though interesting at first, soon grow irksome to one whom education and habits of life have led to different pursuits.

Finally continue to love and respect as your best friends on earth, our only surviving parent and sisters; and you shall see me before June. Farewell! [14]

In this Robert Knox was mistaken. He had, perhaps, misjudged his power to influence the decision of the Army Medical Department, and he had not reckoned on a Kaffir war. He was still in South Africa during the summer of 1820, when the 72nd Regiment, stationed at Port Frederick, helped the Navy to assist the 4,000 English emigrants—asked for by the Governor and known as the "Albany settlers"—to disembark at Algoa Bay. At this time Knox was not with his Regiment but in the Albany district which the settlers had come to colonise, and he must have taken a poor view of them, since it was his misfortune to fall foul of one of the most independent and masterful of them all, Mr Bishop Burnett. Mr Bishop Burnett was not a state-aided emigrant; he had been an officer in the Royal Navy, and he paid his own passage out to South Africa, although travelling in the *Ocean* with one of the subsidised parties with whom he arrived at Grahamstown in May 1820. He was very dissatisfied with what he found there; in the first place he considered that he, and the settlers in general, had been misled about their prospects, and secondly, as a "free-born Englishman"—and he held very firmly to his rights—he was horrified to see the autocratic manner in which the Governor, Lord Charles Somerset, ruled the Colony, and he was prepared to break several lances in defence of the oppressed. Six years later he was to present a petition to the House of Commons setting forth the complaints of the Cape settlers; meanwhile, within weeks of his arrival, he took up the cudgels, almost literally, on behalf of a Boer, Captain Stockenstrom—brother of that Landdrost Stockenstrom under whom Knox had served in the war—who at this time, May 1820, had been, rather childishly perhaps, "sent to Coventry" by his fellow officers of the Cape Corps, a Corps composed mainly of Hottentots and mixed breeds. Dr Knox was then acting surgeon

[14] Henry Lonsdale, *A Sketch of the Life and Writings of Robert Knox, the Anatomist*, London 1870, p. 13.

to this Corps and was evidently believed by Mr Bishop Burnett to be the ringleader of the persecution. There were wheels within wheels in the case. Landdrost Stockenstrom had himself suffered the displeasure of Lord Charles Somerset because he had criticised Lord Charles's son, Captain Henry Somerset, who with very little experience had been made commander of the Cape Corps. Also there seems to be no doubt that there were many people anxious to see Captain Stockenstrom removed from his position as senior Lieutenant of the Corps.

The matter had come to a head in 1819, when the Landdrost wrote that:

> A charge was concocted against him [Capt. Stockenstrom] of stealing a copper coin not worth sixpence, a charge so absurd that it would have disgraced the lowest ginshop, and through an instrumentality that shocked the moral sense of every decent being who knew the relative position of the two men. . . . As I had insisted on a Court of Enquiry it then took place, and resulted in a most ample apology on the part of Captain Henry Somerset in the presence of Captain Harding.

So far, so good, but the young officers of the Regiment had refused to give evidence at the Court of Enquiry, and so Captain Stockenstrom remained "on the black list." The Landdrost, forgetting his old friendship with Knox, wrote bitterly, and ungrammatically, to Lord Charles Somerset that his brother's last state was almost worse than his first, as the proceedings of the Court of Enquiry which had exonerated him had not been made public:

> The world left to put whatever construction it would on the silence which was observed in the quarter whence redress was expected; a Knox in the opportunity of giving whatever colour to his shameful conduct the most refined and plausible cunning could suggest. . . .

This was the position when the invincible Mr Bishop Burnett arrived on the scene and took instant action: he "would not see a man condemned without so much as being informed of what he was accused," and he persisted until another Court of Enquiry sat at Grahamstown, with Major Jackson of the 72nd Regiment as President. Its report was made public on 23 June 1820:

> The Court from all that has come before them do most unequivocally give it as their opinion that Captain Stockenstrom's conduct appears to them to be most highly creditable to him as an Officer and a Gentleman,

and that he has conducted himself through a most painful period of calumny and persecution with feelings of the highest sense of honour and propriety. . . . With regard to Dr Knox the Court look upon his conduct in such a light, that they hope they may be excused from giving an opinion, and refer the Commandant to the above proceedings relative to the calumnies issuing from him.

It is a pity that no record remains extant of any statement made by Knox in defence of his conduct. It is indeed strange that so many of Knox's own statements in moments of crisis have disappeared like this, while those of his detractors have endured to be read by posterity. Whatever he did say at the time evidently made no impression upon Mr Bishop Burnett who, thinking that the censure of the Court did not adequately meet the case, took the law into his own hands and administered a horse-whipping to Dr Knox. Details of this lamentable scene, as indeed of the whole case, are unfortunately few; but the fact that Mr Bishop Burnett in the scuffle received a slight sabre wound suggests that he may not have been one hundred per cent successful in inflicting the punishment.

It was not until 22 October 1820 that Dr Knox left the Cape. Possibly, after this rather undignified finale, it was with few regrets that he stepped on board the brig *Brilliant*, which brought him safely home to England on Christmas Day.

3

Early in the year 1821 Robert Knox was once again established in the Knox family home in Edinburgh, in Nicolson Square, where he probably spent most of his time collating the notes and digesting the information he had acquired during his three years' service in South Africa. He was soon contributing articles on his experiences to the *Edinburgh Medical and Surgical Journal*, and became a member of the Wernerian Natural History Society, to which in March he read a paper on a Kaffir Albino seen by him at the Cape of Good Hope. He had brought three Kaffir skulls home with him; one of these he kept for himself, the others he gave to Dr Monro and Professor Jameson, and according to the

Medical Times, it was Knox who, in these very articles, "gave to the scientific world the first account of the Kaffirs."

The papers that he wrote at this period are noteworthy in that they reveal the variety of his interests, the acuteness of his observations, and the originality of his thought. "Observations on the Taenia solium (tape-worm)" which appeared in the *Edinburgh Medical and Surgical Journal* of July 1821 throw rather a sad light on the diet of the British troops at the Cape: in October 1819 when the men were on active service, this affliction—due to the use of unwholesome or diseased meat—was almost an epidemic, thirty-eight men in one detachment of eighty-six were affected. As a commentary on medical knowledge in the early nineteenth century, it is interesting that Knox thought it worth while to refute a theory that the presence of these parasites could be explained by "any combination of matter converting itself into intestinal worms." Were this true, said Knox (worrying, as always about the origin of life) then

> the origin of men and all other animals would be readily accounted for from a peculiar arrangement and combination of organic molecules placed under peculiar circumstances, and the story of the Python would no longer be a fable.

Among other papers which were published in this same *Journal* one dealt with pericarditis, about which little was known at the time, and from his experiences as an army surgeon Knox also gave his views on "Necrosis and the Regeneration of Bone," even though his ideas were not in harmony with those of some eminent contemporary surgeons.

As he was now an officer on half-pay, Dr Knox could take no further steps towards the advancement of his career without the permission of the Army Medical Department. Here must be recorded the extremely generous treatment which he always received from that Department; not only did he draw his half-pay for another thirteen years, without ever again seeing service, but when he did at last retire, on 2 August 1832, he was given £100 as a commutation payment. So he had no trouble at all when, in September 1821, he asked the Director-General's permission to absent himself from the United Kingdom for one year; his intention being to continue his medical studies in Paris, where he believed that he would find, as indeed he did, great advances in scientific thought. Owing to the greater facilities for anatomical training in France, increasing numbers of British medical students were spending a finishing year there; in 1822 it was reckoned that there were 30 or 40 of them in Paris—the majority Scots. It would appear that Knox had already become a fluent French scholar, for during those trying weeks in Brussels after Waterloo he had observed the disadvantages under which most of the English doctors laboured in not having the French language at their command.

This post-war Paris of 1821, the Paris of the Restoration, when Louis XVIII was king, was everything that Robert Knox had dreamed it would be. "Civilized man," he said, "may perhaps proceed higher even than in Paris, but of this I am not quite sure."[15] In Paris Dr Knox worked at the hospital of La Charité, under Professors Boyer and Roux, and he was, he tells us, by the kindness of Messrs Lherminier and Chomel, given the "utmost facility for Pathological inquiry . . . the mornings of an entire year were occupied in investigating the Pathological Anatomy of cases occurring daily in that Hospital."[16] In Paris he quickly discovered how smoothly, under Government control, the schools of anatomy functioned. In England anyone could open an anatomical school and be responsible for the provision of his own "subjects" for dissection, but as the only "subjects" which could be legally employed were the bodies of convicted murderers, and as the number of these was limited and there were roughly 2,000 medical students in Edinburgh and London alone, there was no alternative to the horrible practice of grave-robbing by medical students and others.

In Paris all the hospitals were run by a public board of management, and there were no private dissecting schools, but two public ones—at the École de la Médicine and the Hôpital de la Pitié—which received their supply of "subjects" in a legal and seemly manner from hospitals and workhouses under the direction of an official, the Chef des travaux anatomiques. The regulations

[15] Races of Men, London 1850, p. 325.
[16] Letter to Lord Provost and Town Council of Edinburgh, 6 Jul. 1837.

were very strictly observed: after death a Mass was said by a priest of the Roman Catholic Church in the hospital chapel, then the body was removed to the "dead room" where it lay for twenty-four hours. If, at the end of that time, it had not been claimed by relatives, it was removed from the hospital in the early hours of the morning, and taken to the anatomy school in "a covered carriage, so constructed as not to attract notice." After dissection the body would be "enveloped in cloth, and conveyed to the nearest place of interment." By this means there was an ample supply of bodies, and exhumation, although a crime punishable under the Penal Code, was in fact unheard of for anatomical purposes. A state of things very different from that existing at home, and one which influenced Knox very deeply. He realised that sooner or later such a scheme would have to be adopted in Britain, and it accustomed him to the idea of using unclaimed bodies in the dissecting-room.

Lonsdale, as a biographer, is extremely unsatisfactory on this period of Robert Knox's life. One of the few details that he records is that on 22 April 1822 Knox was enrolled as a member of a Paris Lodge of Freemasons. At that time Continental Free-masonry was much less innocent than its English counterpart in political and religious matters, and from his subsequent behaviour, Knox at this time must have been an anti-clerical and a Liberal. It is never very easy to pin-point Dr Knox's politics; in England he always seemed to be "agin the Government," no matter what party was in power, and although much of his criticism was sound, it was rarely constructive—his mind usually ranging over less practical problems than those confronting the party politician in his daily round. In France, Knox became a great admirer of Napoleon, and he had the good fortune to hear first hand accounts of him from men who had actually accompanied him on his campaigns.

First and foremost was Baron Larrey, the Emperor's personal friend and Medical Inspector-General, the chief surgeon to his army, who had been through all his battles with him, and had himself been wounded in Egypt and at Waterloo. Larrey was nearly thirty years older than Knox—he was fifty-five in 1821— and had reminiscences of the Revolution as well as of the

Napoleonic wars. His main work, however, was done under Napoleon, for whom he had the greatest admiration. At Aboukir, Larrey had received a sword of honour for valour, many of his amputations having been performed in the field "amid a shower of bullets"; similarly at Borodino he had performed 200 amputations.

Baron Larrey was one of the greatest of military surgeons. That he should have given his friendship to Hospital-Assistant Knox proves that Robert Knox must have been an outstanding figure among the foreign students in Paris in 1821. He was considered not so much a student as an established comparative anatomist with many publications to his credit. He himself states that his work alone served as an introduction to the famous scientists Cuvier, Geoffroy Saint-Hilaire, and De Blainville, with all of whom he maintained a life-long friendship.

It is impossible to over-estimate the influence which Cuvier and Geoffroy had upon him, impossible to comprehend his thought without understanding theirs. Always seeking to "know the unknown," always striving, as in the case of the tape-worms, to discover the origin of life, Knox with youthful optimism thought that he might find in the teaching of these two men the clues he sought to solve the riddles of the Universe. Although today some of the theories expounded by Cuvier and Geoffroy are outmoded, Geoffroy's ideas are always interesting, and Cuvier's work on fossils laid the foundation of modern palaeontology. Charles Darwin linked him with Linnaeus as one of the "two gods" who, after Aristotle, had most inspired him. That science should have advanced with such incredible speed in the last 150 years is due in no small part to pioneers such as these.

Geoffroy was a little younger than Larrey, being forty-nine in 1821; his active service under Napoleon was not on the same scale as Larrey's, but his courage must have been equally great. During the Terror in 1792, on the fatal 2 September, he placed a ladder at midnight against a prison wall and although observed at dawn and a target for bullets, he succeeded in effecting the escape of twelve persons. He was not implicated to the extent of having to withdraw altogether from Paris, and in the following year, although trained as a mineralogist, he was given the Chair of Zoology in the newly constituted Museum of Natural History.

In 1798 Geoffroy was invited by Napoleon to join the Egyptian expedition as a scientific adviser, and Dr Knox, who had so early become an ardent Francophile, seems to have delighted in the tales he told of his encounters with the English when he was trying to safeguard what they considered his loot. The best of all the stories about Napoleon which Geoffroy told to Knox was one which reveals what the Emperor might have achieved had he turned his mind to things of peace instead of war:

> It was in the gardens of Esbekiah, as he was about to quit Egypt, that, conversing with his staff, these memorable words escaped him; they were addressed to Monge,—"I find myself here, conqueror of Egypt, marching in the footsteps of Alexander; but I should have preferred following those of Newton." But Monge replied that Newton had exhausted the field of discovery in physics leaving nothing to those who might follow. "By no means," was the remarkable reply of Napoleon; "Newton dealt with masses of matter, and with their movements; I should have sought in the atoms for the laws by which worlds have been constructed." [17]

Undoubtedly this strengthened, as well it might, Knox's belief in what he called Napoleon's "mighty intellect," although, being no physicist, he did not pursue the fruitful idea.

On his return to Paris from Egypt, Geoffroy became a member of the Academy of Sciences, but in 1808 during the Peninsular War, Napoleon summoned him to Portugal, "with directions to plunder Portugal of whatever she might possess of value or interest in science." "How," asked Knox, "was Geoffroy to act under such circumstances? He was no robber, but a noble, generous, kind-hearted man. Laying it down as a principle that 'the sciences are never at war' he resolved that his mission should be useful to Portugal as well as to France." In this he succeeded so well that, according to his son:

> He plundered the scientific institutions and monasteries of Portugal, but so adroitly, with such urbanity, politesse, and kindly feeling, that the Portuguese themselves not only seemed insensible of the fact, but thanked him for the spoliation.

When he came back from Portugal, Geoffroy was able to resume

---

[17] *Great Artists and Great Anatomists*, p. 119.

PLATE 2

Dr Knox lecturing. A contemporary drawing by Professor Edward
Forbes, famed pupil of Knox.

From *Burke and Hare* by William Roughead, by courtesy of William
Hodge and Company Ltd.

his life as a scientist. He was quickly appointed first Professor of Zoology of the Faculty of Science in the University of Paris, a position which, not having compromised himself in 1814-15, he still held when young Dr Knox arrived in Paris in 1821, and which he continued to hold until his death in 1844.

In his first course of lectures Geoffroy began to expound his views on "transcendental anatomy"—the doctrine of philosophic anatomy which he later published in book form as the *Philosophie Anatomique*. The first part appeared in 1818, the second four years later in 1822, just when Robert Knox was in Paris, and on him it made a tremendous impact.

This doctrine was really an evolutionary one; it was also, at the time, extremely revolutionary. It was nothing less than the "unity of organic composition": nature presenting us with only one plan of construction, the same in principle, but varied in its accessory parts. It accounted for monstrosities by arrested development, and with Goethe, Geoffroy held that there is in nature a law of compensation; if one organ in the body takes on an excess, it is at the expense of another, and if any become superfluous they are retained in rudimentary form. This led to the famous "transcendentalism" in which Geoffroy saw the past, present, and future as an inseparable whole. Although Knox, believing as he did that the "laws of deformation are as regular as the laws of formation,"[18] could not accept all Geoffroy's tenets—especially that of arrested development and, in fact, said that he leaned more to the German ideas on that—the Frenchman's theories did explain to him much that had hitherto been inexplicable, and he enthusiastically described the philosophy as:

> Seeing in Nature one system: and connecting man with the organic world, the existing organic world with the past and with the planetary system, that past system with the universal, endeavouring thus to discover in those relations, the great problem of Man's Creation.[19]

Geoffroy had little training as an anatomist and he might never have reached his conclusions without the work which he had shared with his friend, Baron Cuvier. The two men worked together on scientific papers in the 1790s, Cuvier being the elder

[18] *Great Artists and Great Anatomists*, p. 60.
[19] *Op. cit.*, p. 54.

by three years. In their old age they quarrelled fiercely and publicly over Cuvier's theory of the absolute invariability of species, but in 1821, when Knox met them in Paris, they were still good friends, although their paths had diverged because, unlike Geoffroy, Cuvier had refused Napoleon's invitation to go to Egypt as a scientific adviser. Instead he remained in Paris, working on his theory that extinct animals could be reconstructed from fragmentary remains by practical application of the law of "correlation of growth." He did actually reconstruct the skeletons of more than 160 species of extinct animals, and the museum which he founded for them at the Jardin des Plantes became internationally renowned.

In 1798 Cuvier published his *Tableau eléméntaire de l'histoire naturelle des animaux*. In the following year he became Professor of Natural History in the Collège de France, and in 1800 published his *Leçons d'anatomie comparée*. This gave a great impetus to the study of Comparative Anatomy, and to its use as an essential part of scientific zoology. But it led its author further still. Cuvier studied the fossil bones to be found in the Eocene basin of Paris and, working carefully and laboriously to compare extinct and surviving types, he deduced correctly what they were—the remains of extinct animals, not the bones of giants, nor of men destroyed in the Deluge. This led on to further deductions about the age of the earth and the date of man's arrival upon it, which were difficult to reconcile with orthodox theology. "The natural history of creation," writes Knox triumphantly, "was for the first time explained to man."

In 1812 Cuvier published his *Recherche sur les ossemens fossiles de quadrupèdes*, and followed it in 1817 with his *Règne animal distribué d'après son organisation*, so that, when Dr Knox arrived in Paris in 1821, Cuvier was easily the most eminent of living scientists, and the young student was delighted to sit at the feet of the master, although with some reservations on the risks of reconstructing skeletons from too fragmentary remains. Thirty years later in 1852, in his book *Great Artists and Great Anatomists*, Knox described Cuvier as:

> The greatest anatomist—Descriptive Anatomist—of any age, the scientific man who first, after Aristotle, applied the art of anatomy to general

science. . . . Before Cuvier appeared geology was a farce, a subject of ridicule; cosmogony a myth; the history of creation a tissue of error and absurdities.

Of Cuvier's work on fossils Knox says:

> Thus was opened up to man's view the pristine world; not as we read of it in fabulous histories, the silly imaginings of foolish men, but as Nature made it.

Knox called Cuvier and Geoffroy "the men who have most contributed to the development of the true relation of Anatomy to the Science of Living Beings,"[20] and their ideas affected his whole conception of anatomy, and indeed of life in general. The Robert Knox who returned to Scotland at the end of 1822 was in many ways, particularly in regard to his political and religious principles, ill-suited to the intellectual climate of nineteenth-century Edinburgh. He was now twenty-nine, and he was a man with a mission; he might have been a famous surgeon, for he handled his scalpel with great delicacy and dexterity, but he was a born teacher. He believed that "the enlightenment of the human mind is the highest possible aim of intellect"[21] and he was burning to preach to his compatriots the exciting new gospels he had heard expounded in Paris. His ambition may well have been to make of Edinburgh another Paris—himself its Baron Cuvier.

Dr Knox returned to his native land with perhaps an exaggerated regard for all things French, and a certain contempt for his Scots predecessors and contemporaries—always excepting John Hunter and John Bell. It is possible that Knox bore within him the seed of his own downfall. Aristotle said that there could be no tragedy without some tragic weakness in the hero: the spectacle of "a virtuous man brought from prosperity to adversity" is merely shocking, the tragic hero must be one who is "highly renowned and prosperous, whose misfortune is brought about not by vice or depravity, but by some error or frailty." It may be that the tragic weakness of Knox's character lay in that arrogance of mind which made him estimate too highly the

[20] *Great Artists and Great Anatomists,* Advertisement.
[21] *Op. cit.,* p. 56.

knowledge he had acquired in France—and his own scientific acumen and superiority over his colleagues. That question, however, was for the future. Meanwhile Dr Knox again established himself firmly in Edinburgh, not hearing, as had Sir Charles Bell and others of the profession, the call of the London Medical Schools.

From 1822 to 1824 Knox worked hard to perfect himself in his art. Working alone for seven hours a day, he made the most skilful dissections and "beautiful anatomical preparations." Like other medical men at this time he expended much effort on the elucidation of the action of the eye, then to a great extent unknown. Using comparative anatomy as a guide, Knox dissected the eyes of lizards, fish, chameleons, birds, deer, oxen, and horses; he then examined the eyes of an executed criminal eight hours after death, and read French and German monographs on the subject before writing his own "Observations on the Comparative Anatomy of the Eye" (17 June 1823) for the Royal Society of Edinburgh. Knox was nothing if not thorough, and considering how poor by modern standards his microscopes were, the conclusion he arrived at—that it was a muscle, and not a ligament as was then generally believed, that received the nerves governing vision—was a creditable piece of research. Dr James Moores Ball (an ophthalmic surgeon and author of the book *The Sack-em-up Men*, 1928) gave it as his opinion that "this paper alone should give to Robert Knox a niche in the temple of medical history." He expands this statement by explaining that Dr Knox reached his conclusion by a process of *reasoning*, as the actual microscopic demonstration of the muscular nature of this part of the eye did not take place until 1835.

Knox continued to read papers to the Wernerian Society and to the Royal Society of Edinburgh, of which he was soon elected a Fellow, on subjects as diverse as the cassowary, the beaver, and the electric eel. To the end of his life Knox was perplexed by the problem of the electrical discharges emitted by certain fish. He was to return to it later in another book:

> The gymnotus of Surinam, and the torpedo of the Cape, and one or two more, strike their prey dead by an electrical discharge. To accomplish this, Nature has furnished them with a peculiar apparatus she has denied

to other animals, but the materials called organic are still the same,—it is merely by the arrangements of a few materials that Nature accomplishes so much.

The existence of electric fishes was known to the ancients. Pliny, who collected so much curious nonsense, so many false facts, so many hypotheses which he mistook for facts, knew this fact: viz., that electric fishes exist, and he records it.[22] He knew, also, that people employed the torpedo in the treatment of rheumatism and paralysis; but whilst men are always apt enough to find out some utilitarian application of natural phenomena, no one thought of inquiring into the cause of the phenomenon.

But in 1823 this was, even for Dr Knox, a problem which could wait, for at this time his larger ambition consumed him and the first step towards its realisation was to provide for Edinburgh a proper Museum of Comparative Anatomy which could bear comparison with those he had seen on the Continent. On 2 April 1824, Dr Knox submitted to Mr James Russell, Convener of the Museum Committee, his plan for such a museum for the Royal College of Surgeons of Edinburgh, whose collection at this time was very small:

Dear Sir,

As you were pleased on several occasions to express an interest in some pursuits in comparative anatomy in which I am engaged, and as you are the oldest member of the Royal College of Surgeons and deeply concerned in all that bears upon its interests, I take the liberty of submitting to you the following proposal.

Engaged now for a long period solely in the study of comparative anatomy and physiology, I have felt more than most anatomists the great want of a proper museum and of an osteological collection, without which researches into comparative and human physiology cannot be carried on. But the formation and presentation of such a museum, being altogether beyond the reach of individual means, I have ventured to submit, through you, the following brief sketch of a Plan for the attainment of an object so desirable to science.

Towards the formation of a museum of comparative anatomy I am willing to bestow my whole labour and time, with that energy which the cultivation of a very favourite pursuit naturally gives; the attending expenses of presses, glass, spirits, etc., to be borne by the Royal College of Surgeons. I am, moreover, willing that the Museum so erected be considered as the property of the College, and intended for the use of its

---

[22] Pliny, *Natural History*, Bk. IV, Ch. LXVII.

31

Fellows (as is at present the Pathological collection) reserving to myself during my life-time the use of the Museum for the furtherance of my favourite pursuits and studies.[23]

The moment was opportune, as the Surgeons had already shown themselves anxious to enlarge their existing museum; in 1821 they had made an effort to acquire the collection of Professor Meckel of Halle, and in 1823 they had sent William Cullen to Paris to obtain specimens, but both schemes had proved abortive.

Although at first no agreement was made with Dr Knox by the College, they "encouraged him to commence his labours." By the month of May these were considered "so productive as to make it apparent that the object will not fail of its entire accomplishment from any defect of energy on his part, and will be limited in its progress by nothing short of the wishes or the resources of the College."

Dr Knox had already set up proper shelving and tables, and fitted up an adjoining room as an extension to the Museum, and promised that there should be no interruption to his exertions "until at least the museum shall be in a tolerable state of forwardness." At the next Council meeting of the College certain of his preparations were laid upon the table, so that the Council might judge of his qualifications for the task he proposed to undertake, and the Council judged Dr Knox's qualifications such that they entered into an agreement with him which was very much on the lines of his own proposal, but he had no official position for another six months. Then, following the November half-yearly report of the Curators, describing the "increase in the business of the museum" and the "rapidity and success" with which the Museum of Comparative Anatomy was proceeding, he was in December 1824 appointed

to take charge of the detail of the business of the pathological Museum in co-operation with the keeper and under the direction of the curators appointed by the College; this appointment, like others in the College, shall be for twelve months from September last. £100 salary.

---

[23] Unless otherwise stated the quotations on pp. 32-40 are from the Minute Books of the Royal College of Surgeons of Edinburgh, 1824-6.

It is difficult to assess Dr Knox's income, or to know if he had any private means. All that is certain is that he had his army half-pay, and now this salary from the College of Surgeons, plus, probably, some professional fees, for he did practise a little and acted as assistant at surgical operations. He was lucky also at the outset of his career in being able to live economically at home with his mother and sisters, first at Nicolson Square and then at Newington Place, where it is reasonable to suppose that his five brothers shouldered their share of the expenses. He himself lived simply and his personal expenditure was said to be small, but he spared nothing when in pursuit of knowledge of his art, and when he became the successful owner of an anatomical school and a rich man, he ploughed his profits back. He bought every modern book on anatomy, even costly illustrated ones from the Continent, and in one school session he sacrificed all profit when he spent over £700 in the purchase of "subjects." On his beloved anatomical specimens he would spend money lavishly. He certainly did not possess the usual Scottish virtue of thrift, and saved nothing for the rainy day. Perhaps he had no money sense; and Lonsdale had reason to be worried when he saw him giving fourteen shillings for a brace of grouse, "and in Scotland, too, the great habitat of the bird."

Knox spared neither time, trouble, nor expense in searching for specimens for the new museum:

> He sought the acquaintance of game-keepers and river conservators for the game and fish he wanted for special investigation; and held the Newhaven fish-wives in favour for the opportunities he might gain of the marine fauna of the Forth. To him nearly all the oddities found in the fishing-nets of the neighbouring Firth were brought. He paid well and knew how to divert the fish-wives.[24]

Except for what it could buy for him in the way of anatomical specimens, etc., Knox cared little for money and never aimed at acquiring wealth. He had turned his back without regret on the riches of Africa; now, in March 1825, he conscientiously refused to accept from the College of Surgeons a refund of £21 for the expenses he had incurred the previous month when he had gone to London to inspect Sir Charles Bell's anatomical museum in

[24] Lonsdale, *op. cit.*, p. 27.

33

Great Windmill Street, part of which Sir Charles had offered to the Edinburgh College for £3,000. This journey, Knox said, was a duty he owed to the College:

> The shortness of the period in which I performed the journey to London enabled me to avoid suffering any disadvantages by the neglect of my private affairs: and when I add that excepting the temporary suspension of my anatomical labours I do not know of any inconvenience endured by me on this journey, I am the more convinced of the propriety of declining the remuneration.

Knox estimated that the removal of Bell's museum from London would mean an expenditure of £300, that 1,200 feet of additional shelving would be required and perhaps one moderate-sized glass case costing £120, and the cost of materials for refilling and keeping preparations in order would be £25. The deal went through, and in the summer Dr Knox was sent to London to organise the transport of the collection. The organisation of the packing and transport of the fragile exhibits of an anatomical museum must have taken a tremendous amount of thought and trouble, and Dr Knox was surely an anxious man until he saw them all safely housed in Edinburgh, but he left nothing to chance. He saw the contents of the museum carefully packed into sixty-five cases, loaded on to the smack *Robert Bruce* at London Docks, and on arrival at Leith he had spring carriages, borrowed from the artillery, waiting to transport them into the city.

The Bell Collection, specially rich in surgical pathology, was a very valuable acquisition for the Surgeons' Museum in Edinburgh, where it can still be seen. Charles Bell was a highly skilled artist as well as a surgeon, and Robert Knox, as he unpacked and arranged the contents of the packing cases probably had some bitter moments as he gave pride of place to the great surgeon's sketches of the wounds he had treated after Waterloo. Sketches made up but a small part of the collection, and for Knox it was a labour of love to classify and catalogue the Museum's new possessions. By November he could report that the Bell Collection was unpacked and would in three or four days be ready for examination in temporary accommodation in Nicolson Street. This time he did not refuse the gift of 50 guineas made to him by the College "for his trouble in the removal of the Bell Collection from London."

The College had every reason to be grateful to Dr Knox. He had not allowed the work of the removal and setting up of the Bell Collection to interfere in any way with the "state of forwardness" of the Surgeons' Museum. This was now open to the public on four days a week, and during the six months November 1824—May 1825 he had made 82 preparations (including 4 casts) for exhibition, and was compiling as complete a catalogue as possible: "histories as far as furnished by the gentlemen under whose care the cases occurred have been recorded . . . a short explanation will be attached to each preparation."

The College, however, was not so grateful to Knox that it was prepared to accept him as sole nominee when the post of Conservator of the Museum, at a salary of £150 fell vacant at the end of the year, and the vacancy was actually advertised in the newspapers. The business of the election of the new Conservator came up before the College on 15 May 1826, the very day on which a most excellent Museum Report was also submitted:

> The larger catalogue of the pathological museum has been brought up to January 1826. A descriptive catalogue of Mr Bell's collection has been made and deposited for reference in the Surgeons' Square Museum.
>
> A small additional apartment has been fitted up for the casts, etc. About 500 students have within the last month visited the Museum, and have expressed themselves much gratified with the privilege . . . they have uniformly conducted themselves with the greatest propriety. . . . The zeal, steadiness and talent which Dr Knox has manifested in the different departments of the Museum must be evident to all who have examined it, and appear to the curators eminently to merit the best thanks of the College.

Yet, when the moment came and the President moved that the College should proceed to the election of a Conservator, Dr Robertson moved an amendment that the election be put off "to this day three months to enable candidates with equal or perhaps superior qualifications to Dr Knox to lay their anatomical preparations before the College." This was a fairly ungracious motion in view of Knox's work, but Dr Robertson found a seconder in James Syme, who now comes upon the scene for the first time.

James Syme in 1826 was twenty-seven years of age, Knox thirty-three, and although Syme had not been an army surgeon his education had otherwise followed very closely the same pattern as that of Knox: Edinburgh High School, two years at Edinburgh University, assistant and demonstrator to John Barclay, a year's study in Paris, and then assistant in Liston's anatomical school in Edinburgh. When Liston began to devote himself entirely to surgery Syme took over the school in 1823, and he continued to run it for three years, finding ever increasing difficulty in obtaining "subjects," which may well have generated suspicion and jealousy of his more successful rival, Robert Knox. By 1826, however, Syme had quarrelled with Liston, abandoned anatomy for surgery, and opened his own school in pure Surgery. Syme was, without doubt, a most brilliant surgeon but a most quarrelsome man; indeed it has been said that the only member of his profession with whom he did not quarrel was his son-in-law, Lister. Comrie, the Scots medical historian, calls Syme "acrimonious," he refers to his quarrels with Liston, Lizars, Simpson, and Miller and recalls that "he also quarrelled with his fellow members of the General Medical Council, and even on one occasion, in regard to the law of evidence, with the judge who was trying a case in which he was a witness."

This then, was the man who was to become Knox's implacable enemy, but on this occasion his machinations failed and the College did not accept the amendment postponing the election of their Conservator. Mr George Bell moved the appointment of Dr Knox as Conservator, saying that "it was quite unnecessary for him to pronounce any eulogism on Dr Knox as his abilities were well known to all the members present," and this was seconded by Mr Wishart. But Dr Robertson had not yet abandoned his opposition. He next seconded a motion by Dr Macintosh that

> Dr Robert E. Grant who had produced most ample testimonials of his qualification for the office, and whom he knew to be equally distinguished for his abilities and zeal in his profession and for the utmost urbanity and modesty of manner, should be appointed Conservator.

The sting of that motion lay in its tail, and Knox must have had several anxious moments, for it was only too obvious that his election was not a foregone conclusion; but, when the vote was taken he found himself elected Conservator, with a majority of twenty-six over Dr Grant—thirty-four votes to eight. For the first time his colleagues had shown him the red light of their antagonism, but it was a warning which he failed to take.

One of Knox's first official duties was to visit London to receive the remaining portion of the Bell Museum, for which additional accommodation had been found in Edinburgh by the purchase of John Bell's house in Surgeons' Square. It is interesting that, on his return, Knox was voted £25 for his extra trouble, and the thanks of the College for his activity and zeal. The fierce light which has played upon Robert Knox, the Anatomist, has tended to obscure Robert Knox, the Museum Conservator, and far too little has been said about his work in this field in which he was also a pioneer. His ability to run two such careers concurrently shows his power of concentration and his capacity for hard work.

On 2 March 1825, almost at the moment of his first visit to London to inspect the Bell Collection, Knox signed a deed of co-partnership with his old tutor, Dr John Barclay. Since Knox had been his pupil, Barclay had gone from success to success; he had moved from his house in High School Yards to No. 10 Surgeons' Square, a three-story house with arches and pillars, which stood between Old Surgeons' Hall and the old Hall of the Medical Society. Now, in his sixty-fifth year, with an average class of 300 pupils, he wished to enjoy greater leisure, and in Robert Knox he saw just the man he wanted to succeed him, "a person of precision, method and expertness, a growing naturalist, and an excellent human and comparative anatomist."[25]

The contract concluded between the two men suited them both admirably; Knox agreeing to relieve Barclay "of the whole labour in every branch of the Institution whatsoever during the continuance of the co-partnership," subject to a proviso that Barclay could undertake any part agreeable to himself. Another clause, which may show the trend of his mind, made provision for the eventuality of Knox obtaining a professorship at any university. Before the session began Knox hastily took steps to

[25] Lonsdale, *op. cit.*, p. 44.

become a member of the Royal College of Surgeons of Edinburgh in order to be an officially recognised lecturer. On 18 March he was examined by the College authorities in Anatomy and Surgery; on 2 April in Materia Medica, Chemistry, and Pharmacy; on 19 April on his paper (52 pages 8vo) "On the Causes and Treatment of Lateral Curvature of the Human Spine," which malady he attributed to the "direst results of civilization—arising from an abuse of sedentary employments, an excessive manufacturing population, and a total neglect of the physical education of youth." On this occasion, as recorded in the Minutes of the College:

> He appeared, produced his burgess ticket, was examined on his essay and was found duly qualified. Therefore and in consideration of his having paid £250 Sterling as his entry money with the Clerks and Officers fees, the Royal College and Incorporation of Surgeons of the City of Edinburgh have admitted and received the said Dr Knox to be a free Surgeon Apothecary in Edinburgh, and to enjoy all the liberties and privileges of the said Royal College and Incorporation, whereupon he signed the declaration appointed for entrants, and took his seat as a member.

The surgeons seem to have thought well of Barclay's choice of a successor. Sir George Ballingall, in his *Life of Dr Barclay*, written in 1827 (*i.e.*, a year before the Burke and Hare storm broke) refers to Dr Knox as:

> already well known to his profession as an assiduous and successful cultivator of anatomical science, and who has shown himself, by his lectures, both on Human and Comparative Anatomy, so well qualified to support the character of the establishment to which he has succeeded.

He had succeeded to it sooner than might have been expected. Barclay gave an introductory lecture to the 1825-6 session at Surgeons' Square and then went into retirement, which he enjoyed for a matter of months only, as he died on 21 August 1826. He bequeathed his museum to the Royal College of Surgeons of Edinburgh, but in his will he nominated Knox as one of the trustees and in a further clause stated:

> Dr Knox is recommended to be continued and appointed Keeper and Conservator of this Museum while under the charge of the Trustees, and after delivery to the Royal College of Surgeons to be by them continued and appointed Keeper and Conservator for life.

Although Dr Knox was legally entitled to retain possession of the museum until Whitsunday 1828 he "very handsomely" handed it over at once to the College "with the exception of some preparations for the illustration of his lectures." It was a very valuable collection, containing very fine vascular preparations and also specimens in Comparative Anatomy, including the skeletons of an elephant and a camel.

So, at the start of the session 1826-7 Knox found himself in sole possession of Barclay's anatomical school in Surgeons' Square. Some men might have felt themselves unequal to the task of following so great a teacher as Barclay, but Robert Knox was not of their number. "Knox," says Lonsdale, "was more than a successor to his distinguished master; he was himself, and soon came to be designated by his class 'Knox primus et incomparabilis'."

Knox knew that he had a greater message than his master. Barclay had provided beautiful dissections, sound surgical practice, and accurate knowledge of the human frame: Knox was prepared to do this and more. Of Anatomy he wrote:

> Anatomy is not a science, but merely a mechanical art, a means towards an end. It is pursued by the physician and surgeon for the detection of disease, and the performance of operations; by both to discover the functions of the organs; and by the philosopher with the hope of detecting the laws of organic life, the origin of living beings, and the transcendental laws regulating the living world in time and space.[26]

Knox would not make his pupils dissect for dissection's sake alone. Once they had become proficient and learned the underlying principle, he would make them compare human anatomy with that of birds and animals, and trace the similarity between them which proved to him the validity of the French idea of the "organic whole." He showed them the rudimentary organs in the human embryo, and using the specimens in his museum, traced their progressive evolution. He had fossils, also, to demonstrate Cuvier's palaeontology, which proved how short in time was man's existence on earth. This was the strength of Knox's appeal to youth; it had novelty in revealing some of the secrets of the past and it was forward-looking. Believing, as he

[26] *Great Artists and Great Anatomists*, p. 141.

did, that the discovery of truth was not only the "greatest achievement of human intellect"[27] but also the "only rational end of human existence"[28] Knox was certain that one day science would reveal the mystery of life itself. Meanwhile his aim was to instil into his students "a desire to know the unknown; a love of the perfect; an aiming at the universal."[29] It was a high ideal.

4

Dr Knox had three rules of health; temperance, early rising, and frequent change of linen. If the last seems to us something to be taken for granted, it must be remembered that it was not always so. In the early nineteenth century even surgical cleanliness was not a commonplace, for Lister did not introduce his antiseptic system until 1865, and in 1825 it was quite customary for the surgeon to wear at the operating-table "an old blood-stained coat, with a bunch of silk ligatures threaded through one of the button-holes, ready for use." Sir Astley Cooper, when summoned on one occasion to attend King George IV, tarried neither to change his blood-stained shirt nor wash his blood-stained hands and was then surprised that the fastidious monarch should have "looked displeased" on receiving him. The surprise of Edinburgh can therefore be imagined when Knox arrived to give his anatomical and physiological lectures clad in the height of fashion: "with spotless linen, frill and lace and jewellery . . . standing in a class-room amid osseous forms, cadavera, and decaying mortalities, he was a sight to behold, and one assuredly never to be forgotten." A sight, nevertheless, which sober Edinburgh found somewhat suspect.

To be rather more precise, Dr Knox usually wore a dark puce or black coat, a showy vest, often richly embroidered with purple, and delicately-plaited cambrics, a high cravat, held in place by a diamond ring, a prominent shirt collar, dark trousers and shining boots. His first action on entering his lecture-room

[27] *Great Artists and Great Anatomists*, p. 56.
[28] *Op. cit.*, p. 1.
[29] *Op. cit.*, p. 22.

was to place his watch and seals upon the table and survey his class, and "after each division of his subject he would readjust his spectacles, draw up the waist-band of his trousers—he wore no braces—and then, presenting a steady front to his class, resume his prelection." In other words he knew exactly what to do to break the monotony of his lecture, to attract the attention of his students, and if, as was possible, he wished to distract them from concentration on his face—"Old Cyclops" had no illusions about the ravages wrought upon it by the small-pox—what better distraction than a showy waistcoat and a gold chain or two?

There is no doubt that Dr Knox gave minute attention to the presentation of himself and his lectures before the public. His contemporaries were amused when they discovered that he had actually rehearsed one of them in the lecture-theatre; they were equally amused when he was found having a curling-tongs applied to one of his few remaining locks of hair. But have we of today any right to be so amused? The television lecturer adopts both procedures as part of his routine, and what a TV personality Robert Knox would have made! From his first entrance into the hall Knox had his movements well planned:

> Some lecturers walk unconcernedly to their desk and read off-hand; some are condescending, others are brusque in manner. . . . The exits and entrances of Knox were alike graceful and exceedingly characteristic; nor did he for a moment during the hour of lecture lose his suave demeanour and high respect for his class as a body of gentlemen.[30]

The small-pox which had ruined his features had at least left him with great grace of movement, which accompanied by rapid gesture, made memorable his demonstrations of his anatomical exhibits. In addition Knox was the possessor of a particularly attractive voice, and that, combined with his command of the English language, enabled him to put across the matter of his lecture in a most felicitous manner. He never read from notes and was never accused of giving a dull lecture.

In the *Edinburgh Courant* the reviewer of Lonsdale's biography

[30] Lonsdale, *op. cit.*, p. 126.

of Knox gives one of the best first-hand accounts of Knox's style as a lecturer:

> The prevailing element of Knox's oratory was a facile, soft, insinuating power. . . . Never was there a more ready or fluent man than Knox. These traits we can illustrate from a statement of his own, since he said of himself on one occasion: "Goodsir's difficulty often is to find a word; my difficulty is to choose from the words that offer themselves." And his readiness, whether in repartee, or in adapting his speech to circumstances, was more like an electric play of inspiration than anything else.

Yet in spite of such fluency, Knox, on the testimony of another of his students (Sir Benjamin Ward Richardson), knew when to stop:

> Knox was a genius in the art of teaching. He certainly made all matters clear, and that in such a way that his hearers, in listening to him, were reminded of something they had formerly acquired. He was also an eloquent man, was never at a loss for a word, and never spoke a word too much. One of my colleagues said that as a lecturer Knox was "warm and comfortable" and there could not be a better description.

For Robert Knox anatomical science was the most important thing in life. His infectious enthusiasm convinced because he had such belief in himself and his teaching that he inspired confidence. His students held him in the highest respect and honour, and he put before them his own lofty conception of the benefit to mankind of a complete and correct knowledge of anatomy, and also its more practical aspect:

> To the question frequently put as to the utility of minute anatomy I reply that this invaluable knowledge will enable you to reject many idle speculations in physiology and pathology daily offered you; by it you may at least check, if not destroy, empiricism, and combat rash surgery, come from whom it may.

Knox took a warm individual interest in his students, calling each one of them by his Christian name and criticising their work in a good-natured way:

> When Knox sat down to instruct a pupil it was in a masterly fashion; the fine sweep of the scalpel, the line of precision, the unfolding of tissues, and finally a clear demonstration with a fund of information, physiological, surgical, and pathological. When he saw the pupil slashing away at the muscles of a part, he touched the young man's shoulder and said: "Ah,

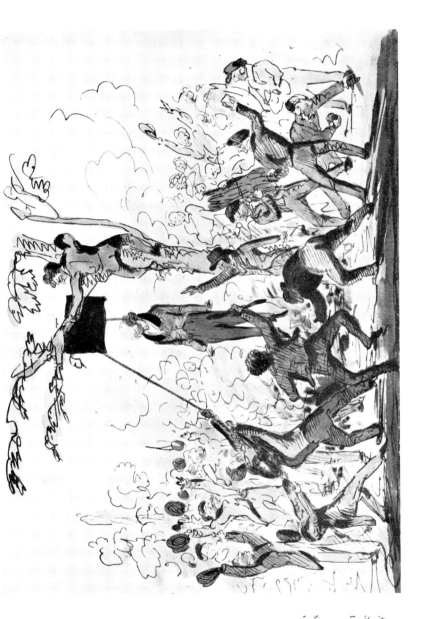

PLATE 3

The Newington Auto-da-Fé, showing the burning of Knox's effigy.

From a watercolour sketch in *Noxiana*, by courtesy of the Trustees of the National Library of Scotland.

sir! I see you are dissecting for the sake of the bones; would it not be as well to pick up a few facts as to the attachments and uses of these muscles before you reach the skeleton?"[31]

If the work were finished in time, Knox would make the last half-hour of the day pleasant and informal, as standing with his back to the fire, he would discuss with his class the current theological and scientific questions.

Soon Dr Knox's success became phenomenal. Barclay had had to lecture twice daily; Knox had to give his daily lecture three times over, often consecutively. It was a great strain, but Knox did not consider his personal convenience so long as the cause which he had at heart was advanced. He set himself to work a fourteen-hour day, from 7 a.m.—9 p.m.; his simple meals were brought to the Museum, "coffee and eggs at ten in the morning, soup or Scotch kail containing meat and vegetables at five, but no stimulant." The work that he was doing at the Museum at this time was very considerable. As the various collections and other donations were added, new accommodation had continually to be found, but by November 1826, it was possible for him to report that the exhibits in Nicolson Street and Surgeons' Hall had been moved to new premises, where they formed one museum of pathological anatomy. The new premises consisted of John Bell's house in Surgeons' Square. It was opened to the public at the beginning of the winter session, but very soon it became evident that, even with this addition, the accommodation was still inadequate to display properly the recently acquired Barclay collection.

By the summer of 1828 the overcrowding of the Museum had reached serious proportions, and in August, to add to Knox's dilemma, the architect, Mr Playfair, reported Surgeons' Hall to be structurally unsafe and it became essential to remove the anatomical museum and part of the Barclay collection still housed in it. Although this occurred in the fateful autumn of 1828 when Knox's anatomical class was at the peak of its fame, he immediately, with the assistance of his brother Fred and one or two others, set to work to effect the removal and by dint of what he called "incessant labour," carried it through without damage

[31] Lonsdale, *op. cit.*, p. 159.

or loss. On 29 October 1828, he sent in his report to the Curators, stating that he hoped the arrangements would be completed by Tuesday, 4 November, when the re-organised Museum should be open to the public, the pathological collection and the best of the Barclay exhibits in John Bell's house, and the larger skeletons and the anatomical museum in another more recently rented house.

The Curators of the Museum submitted the report of their Conservator to the Council with a few introductory remarks:

> The Curators conceive that they do no more than justice to their Conservator (whose labours during the last three months have been most arduous) in simply submitting to you his own statement of the manner in which he has disposed of the valuable collections under his care after the Report of Mr Playfair had rendered it necessary to abandon the Hall.[32]

Dr Knox had said in his report that these changes in the position of all the museums exceeded all his former labours as Conservator. To anyone with any experience of the removal and re-housing of museum exhibits, these labours appear not only arduous but herculean. He was no ordinary man who could do all this and simultaneously teach the largest anatomical class that had ever assembled in Britain. Only afterwards, perhaps, Dr Knox may have reflected that some of those long hours in the museum might have been more wisely employed in obtaining a greater knowledge of his suppliers of "subjects."

In this same winter session of 1828-9 there were inscribed in Dr Knox's books the names of no less than 504 students—"all in their own hand-writing"[33] he later commented sardonically. Students from other faculties often attended, and the sons of the Scottish nobility also patronised Knox; his pupil Lord Glenorchy presented him with the skeletons of wild cats for his museum; another pupil, the future Marquis of Breadalbane, always entertained him to dinner at the Palace of Holyroodhouse during his annual visits there, and Knox, according to Lonsdale, "liked breeding and princely feasts . . . he dearly loved the attention of a lord of ancestral name and in the possession of rich perquisites. Democracy, with Knox, as with many others, was very well in

[32] R.C.S. (Ed) Minutes, 11 Nov. 1828.
[33] Letter to Lord Provost and Town Council, 6 Jul. 1837.

44

the abstract." This may be true in so far that Dr Knox quite frankly admitted a dislike of what he called in his superior way the *canaille*, or quoting the earlier Knox, "the rascal multitude," and he may easily have given the impression of being a "most superior person," for he certainly did not suffer fools gladly. But when due allowance is made for a sprinkling of the nobility at his lectures, the main body of Knox's students was bona-fide medical. Soon two-thirds of all the medical students in Edinburgh—and the most brilliant, as their later careers were to show—were attending his classes, and this did not make him more of a favourite with his professional rivals. Visitors from the south did not consider that their stay in Edinburgh had been complete unless they had been to Surgeons' Square. Country practitioners, living at a distance of twenty miles or more from the capital, thought nothing of riding into Edinburgh, even through November frost and snow, to attend Knox's "Introductory." There is no doubt that such success aroused jealousy, especially on the other side of the University wall, where Alexander Monro, *tertius*, was still Professor of Anatomy. But just then Dr Knox was too busy to care or perhaps even to notice.

Dr Knox "seemed to live to lecture," and not content with a five-day week, he undertook a series of "Saturday Lectures." These were public lectures which he gave for an hour at Old Surgeons' Hall on Saturday mornings to an audience more advanced than that which usually occupied his school benches. It was one of the best services he could have rendered to Anatomy, which at that time was the Cinderella of medical science and in much need of popularising, confused as the subject was in the public mind.

Dr Knox was not unaware of the problem he had thus set himself in lecturing to a highly educated, yet not scientific, audience. His main difficulty, he said, was "to place the great physiological principles regulating human and other living beings before them in intelligible form."[34] In this he succeeded admirably. When he spoke on Saturdays of Comparative and General Anatomy, Zoology, and Ethnology, he spoke to his adult audiences from his own wide culture: his medical and classical

---

[34] *Races of Men*, London 1850, p. 7.

45

learning, his historical knowledge, his acquaintance with modern Africa and contemporary France, all this he laid before his listeners in clear and pithy terms. He would explain, as simply as possible, the great importance of Cuvier's work on fossils, which could give a clue to the date of the creation of the earth and its inhabitants. He would expound Geoffroy's "transcendental anatomy" which had extended Cuvier's vision of the past to include the future, and so connected man "with all life, past, present and to come."[35] And to this Knox added his own comment:

> The idea of new creations, or of any creation saving that of living matter, is wholly inadmissible. The world is composed of matter, not of mind. The circumstances giving rise, then, to the specializations of animal and vegetable forms, giving them a permanency of some thousand years, are as yet unknown to us, and may for ever remain so; but that is no reason why they should not be inquired into.[36]

These ideas may not seem very revolutionary today, but they must be seen in perspective against their contemporary historical background: Sir Charles Bell accepting Paley's *Evidences of Christianity* without questioning "final causes"; Bibles still being printed with Bishop Ussher's chronology which fixed the date of the Creation at 4004 B.C. Knox's creed was very different:

> The universal system of nature must have been formed by fixed, un-alterable, eternal laws; it is still regulated by them. The globe we inhabit, and all that it contains, forms no exception to this. . . . Out of elemental bodies all living forms arise. Their course and existence are fixed and determined. . . . The law of this progression has not been discovered, but man plays a part in it. What that part is cannot even be guessed at, in consequence of the failure of civilization to better man's condition on the globe. . . . Some writers have confounded the theory of development with the theory of progress. They are quite different.[37]

It is easy to see why Knox was unpopular with the doctors and the clergy, but it is also easy to understand how he roused the enthusiasm of his audiences. He had a light touch and an easy style, and his knowledge of the world and its history seemed

[35] *Races of Men*, London 1850, p. 11.
[36] *Op. cit.*, p. 444.
[37] *Op. cit.*, p. 477, n. 13.

illimitable. He could fire the imagination of his hearers at will. No wonder that the Saturday audiences, when Dr Knox had been more than usually eloquent and witty, "stood up *en masse* as he bowed his exit, and waved hats and handkerchiefs, crying "Bravo! bravo! Knox for ever and one cheer more!"

In one of his essays Max Beerbohm divided mankind into two classes, natural hosts and guests. On the rare occasions when he could leave his work Dr Knox was pre-eminently a host, and on the evenings when he chose to relax and entertain guests at his "acknowledged" residence (the adjective is Lonsdale's) at 4 Newington Place, the parties were assured of success. There, with Miss Mary Knox, his eldest sister, fourteen years older than himself, acting as hostess, Dr Knox gave

> dinners and evening parties in excellent style and with good musical accompaniments. Everybody was made happy at Knox's fireside. The intellectual and the humorous could not fail to be pleased with mine host's talk and jokes that always set the table in a roar. Knox at home was Knox triumphant: his cheery words and affable manner were as exhilarating as draughts of champagne.

The South African stories doubtless figured largely in his repertoire, and there is no doubt that Knox himself enjoyed the evenings. Besides enjoying the good company Knox was a great music lover and seems to have favoured the German and Italian schools, with Schubert and Rossini as his best loved composers; he often compared them with the English, to the disadvantage of the latter. Scottish dance music on the contrary, appealed to him, and when a Highland Reel was struck up he would join in with a graceful bow and "snap his fingers con-sonantly with the emphatic notes." Women found him a pleasant companion; his courtesy and easy manner outweighed his lack of good looks, "Knox at length came to be pronounced 'a delightful' or 'charming' person by the prettiest of women."

So much for the good cheer of Knox's "acknowledged" residence. At Knox's unacknowledged residence, so it was said, "Mrs Grundy left no card!" There he was supposed to live, apparently very happily, with an ever-increasing family and a woman whom nobody ever met and whose name nobody ever knew, but Lonsdale, mentioning only her "inferior rank," says,

47

"Knox inconsiderately put shackles to his social progress" by secretly marrying her at the age of thirty-one, in 1824. This is confirmed by Knox's son-in-law, J. Syme Wilsone, who in 1863, drew the attention of the editor of the *Lancet* to an error in its obituary of his father-in-law; the date of Dr Knox's "contract of marriage,"[38] wrote Syme Wilsone, was 1824, not 1832, as stated in the *Lancet*.

Victorian biographers were apt to pursue a "sealed lips" policy when their heroes did not live up to their own moral standards. In 1867, in a biographical sketch of another Edinburgh man, an ex-Lord Chancellor, Thomas, Lord Erskine, the author stated briefly that Erskine's "former fame was obscured by an unhappy second marriage with a Miss Sarah Buck, and certain eccentricities of conduct which were very incompatible with his age and station." Sarah Buck was, in fact, a domestic servant, and Erskine, at the age of sixty-eight, married her at Gretna Green in October 1818, after she had borne him two children. Three years later she sued him for a separation in what became a very sordid law-suit, and in 1823 the poor old man died. In this case, where a famous and brilliant man had, in his dotage, fallen into evil ways, the biographer was clearly, from kindly motives, putting the best gloss he could upon the facts.

In the case of Dr Robert Knox there seems to be no reason at all, except pure snobbery, for the veil of secrecy which surrounds his wife. There were no illegitimate children in the Knox family; Knox's son-in-law in his letter to the *Lancet*, giving the date of Dr Knox's "contract of marriage" as 1824, had made that abundantly clear, as his own wife Mary, Dr Knox's eldest child, was thirty-three when she died in 1858. It seems a pity, then, not to know more about Mrs Knox, the woman who must have been Knox's sole support and comforter in the dark days of 1829. Lonsdale believed that Knox imperilled his career by this *mésalliance*, and indeed, if the disparity in social degree were as great as he implies, Dr Knox perhaps did a service to his wife when he protected her from the barbs of class-conscious Edinburgh society.

Yet there seems to be another side to the story. Although

[38] *Lancet*, 10 Jan. 1863.

48

Lonsdale is so reticent about Mrs Knox he never suggests that Knox was other than a model husband and father, and the question arises as to whether Knox himself was as secretive about his wife as was his biographer; or indeed if he ever had an "unacknowledged" address. In the Census of Scotland, taken on 7 June 1841, the household in residence at 4 Newington Place, the so-called "acknowledged" address, consisted of three Knoxes —Robert, Mary, and Jessie, aged respectively 49, 45, and 41; two juveniles, Thomas Birnie and Janet Deorra, the latter a maid-servant, and an Englishman, William Hunter, presumably a student. Admittedly Knox's children were not there that night, but what is perhaps more important, neither was his sister Miss Mary Knox, the reputed hostess at No. 4, who in 1841 would have been sixty-two years old. Unfortunately the Census Returns of 1841 did not include "particulars of relationship to Head of Family and Condition as to Marriage" (all that was required was "occupation" and Knox gave his as "Professor of Anatomy" and the other adults were entered as "independent") but this Mary Knox who was four years younger than Knox— her age is given as forty-five and her place of birth as "Scotland" —who was at 4 Newington Place on the night of 7 June 1841, can surely be none other than his wife. We know that she was to die in that same year, and it must be more than coincidence that a Mrs Mary Knox of the very same age, forty-five, should have been buried in Greyfriars Churchyard on 1 September, her death having taken place in the Infirmary.

Dylan Thomas, when he was writing his film script about Dr Knox, *The Doctor and the Devils*, also found himself faced with this problem of the elusive Mrs Knox, but as he was writing for the screen he solved it by inventing a devoted house-maid to play the part. However that may be, Dylan Thomas did make the point that Knox, when he married, must have married wholly for love, and it seems unreasonable to blame him for that.

5

The 1826-7 session of his School of Anatomy, the first on his own, might seem to have marked the summit of Knox's ambition. Sir James McGrigor, Director-General of the Army Medical Department, who still kept an eye on his half-pay officer, then wrote to congratulate him: "You know I never doubted your success as a teacher, I rejoice to know that it has been so complete." His future course, too, looked as though it were set fair for years. Yet by the end of the year 1826 Knox was faced with difficulties on a scale which had never worried Barclay. His very success was a problem; somehow sufficient "subjects" had to be provided for the instruction of his hundreds of pupils—and Knox was determined that those pupils should never have anything less than the best instruction. His advertisement for the "Anatomy and Physiology" courses stated that: "each of these courses will as usual comprise a full Demonstration on fresh Anatomical Subjects." For the "Practical Anatomy and Operative Surgery" courses, from October to July, arrangements had been made "to secure as usual an ample supply of Anatomical Subjects." The fee for the first course was £3 5s, and £2 9s for the second, "an additional Fee of Three Guineas includes Subjects." There was no going back on that.

In 1826 Dr Knox was not the only extra-mural teacher of anatomy. Robert Liston, who had also been a pupil of Barclay's had started lecturing in 1818, and although he had abandoned teaching for surgery, his class was taken over by James Syme in 1823 and later by Cullen. Another anatomist and surgeon who was teaching at this time was John Lizars; there was also John Aitkin. There was room for them all, because at last dissection had become a compulsory subject for both the Edinburgh M.D. and College of Surgeons' degrees; this meant that the new demand for the teaching of practical anatomy created an excessive demand for bodies to dissect. This, however, was not a new problem in Edinburgh, a fact which is too often forgotten when the topic of body-snatching comes under discussion. Too often people ignorant of the facts speak of Dr Knox as though he were the prime instigator and organiser of the whole infamous trade, whereas, in fact, it had been going on for at least a hundred years, since the early eighteenth century. By 1826 the problem had changed in degree but not in kind.

As early as the year 1505 the Town Council of Edinburgh granted the petition of the Corporation of Barber-Surgeons

> that we may have anis in the year ane condampnit man after he be deid, to make anatomea of, quairthrow we may heif experience, ilk ane to instruct utheris, and we sall do suffrage for the soule.

In 1694 the Town Council went further and made a gift to an individual, Alexander Monteith, at his request,

> of those bodies that dye in the correction-house and of the bodies of foundlings that dye upon the breast.

and to the Surgeons they gave:

> the bodies of foundlings who dye betwixt the time that they are weaned and their being put to schools or trades; also the dead bodies of such as are stiflet in the birth, which are exposed, and have none to owne them; as also the dead bodies of such as are felo de se, and have none to owne them, likwayes the bodies of such as are put to death by sentence of the magistrate, and have none to owne them.

Notwithstanding these arrangements, by 1711 there was a scarcity of material for dissection, and also a series of complaints about the robbing of graves in Greyfriars churchyard which the Surgeons dismissed as "a scandalous report, most maliciously spread about the town." Yet in 1725 they had to issue another almost similar declaration because country people and servants in the towns were frightened of being "attacked and seized by Chirurgeons' apprentices in order to be dissected." There had also been a riot in Edinburgh against body-snatching which had caused Alexander Monro, *primus*, then Professor of Anatomy in the city and college of Edinburgh, to remove himself and his anatomical specimens for safety's sake from Surgeons' Hall to the University.

That the public had some reason for uneasiness had been shown in the previous year, 1724, when there had been a free fight near Musselburgh between some surgeon-apprentices and the friends of a woman who had just been hanged as a criminal, for the possession of her body. To the confusion of all, the "corpse" came to life in the midst of the struggle, and lived on for another thirty years—always being known as "half-hangit Maggie Dickson."

After this scandal supply seemed to keep up with demand until the beginning of the nineteenth century, when the large numbers of John Barclay's students produced a demand so unprecedented that it strained all sources of local supply, and Barclay himself sent to London for "subjects." This was not by any means an ideal arrangement because they came by sea, and although marked "perishable goods," were rarely in good condition on arrival. When, therefore, large prices could be obtained for bodies, a lucrative field lay open to the "Resurrectionists," those men, who unlike the surgeon-apprentices, had no interest whatever in medicine, but only in what they could make out of their dangerous, unpleasant, and illegal trade of grave-robbing. They were really the scum of the city; Sir Astley Cooper described them as "the lowest dregs of degradation."

Of their methods Sir Robert Christison has given a detailed contemporary account:

> The time chosen in the dark winter nights was, for the town church-yards, from 6-8 o'clock, at which later hour the churchyard watch was set, and the city police also commenced their night rounds. A hole was dug down to the coffin only where the head lay—a canvas sheet being stretched around to receive the earth, and to prevent any of it spoiling the smooth uniformity of the grass. The digging was done with short, flat, dagger-shaped implements of wood, to avoid the clicking noise of iron striking stones. On reaching the coffin two broad iron hooks under the lid, pulled forcibly up with a rope, broke off a sufficient portion of the lid to allow the body to be dragged out, and sacking was heaped over the whole to deaden the sound of the cracking wood. . . . The whole process could be completed in an hour, even though the grave might be 6 ft. deep, because the soil was loose, and the digging was done impetuously by frequent relays of active men. Transference over the churchyard wall was easy in a dark evening, and once in the street, the carrier of the sack drew no attention at so early an hour.

The Resurrectionists' business remained seemly as long as Monro and Barclay between them had the monopoly of anatomical teaching in Edinburgh, because they had some sort of gentleman's agreement about the apportioning of the spoils.

But when Robert Liston came on the scene as a teacher of anatomy with an equal interest in "subjects," competition ran high, and rival gangs would fight each other even in the church-yard.

By this time there were again amateur as well as professional body-snatchers, for the most intelligent of the students were angry that they should be penalised in the pursuit of their studies by lack of material, a state of things which they felt to be grossly unfair when the medical schools on the Continent were not similarly handicapped by their governments. They thought it no shame to be body-snatchers in a good cause, and indeed one of the most successful of them all was Robert Liston himself who brought a certain *panache* to the occupation.

Few of those who looked at a remarkable skeleton (exhibit No. 3,389 in the College of Surgeons' Museum, Edinburgh, presented by Robert Liston) had any idea of its even more remarkable history:

A country lad whose disease had excited large interest, and upon whose case numerous medical men had been consulted, at length succumbed to hydrocephalus, and his body was buried in the exposed cemetery of a fishing burgh on the shores of the Firth of Forth. Having strong sus-picions of the doctors, the friends of the deceased engaged trustworthy watchers of his grave—men who for night after night, and week after week, resisted every overture of bribes and whisky offered them by the Resurrectionists. The agents of Monro and Barclay and others were all intent upon what in the language of the schools was termed "a rare osteological specimen"; money was abundantly lavished and every artifice and intrigue put in force to obtain the subject, but all to no purpose. Weeks had gone over and the excitement of the contest between the "watchers" and the besieging force of Resurrectionists had passed away, when one evening at dusk two well-dressed gentlemen, smoking their cigars, drove up in a dog-cart to the chief hostelry of the little burgh: they alighted, and requested that their horse might be taken care of for an hour.

The "whip-hand" gentleman told the ostler that he expected a livery servant to bring a parcel for him, which could be put in the box part of the conveyance, to which the key was attached. In a short time a man in smart livery came to the stable-yard, deposited a bag under the seat of the dog-cart, pocketed the key and walked off,—"a canny silent man, or dull o' hearing."

Whilst the unknown gentlemen were trotting homewards at full speed, the watchers of the night were approaching their post of duty. As usual on entering the cemetery, they looked at the grave to see that all was right; but to their astonishment found that it had been disturbed; nay, more that the coffin was broken, and that the body had gone! What! abstracted in day-light—impossible, yet too true! The reader will have surmised that the "dog-cart gentlemen" were the depredators and most expert ones. . . . Availing themselves of the twilight just before the watchers appeared on the ground, they succeeded in disinterring the body and carrying it off in 30 minutes.

The "whip-hand gentleman" was of course, Robert Liston.

In the lower parts of Edinburgh, in the Cowgate and Canongate, there were murkier doings in which surgeons and students did not participate. There the most villainous of the Resurrection men—"Stupe" and "Spune," "Merry Andrew," and "Moudie-warp" (Mole), for they rarely used their own names—in the teeming tenements and sordid lodging-houses of the Old Town would listen to the last mutterings of the friendless dying, and make what sense of them they could, in order to reappear suitably disguised as relatives to claim the body. "Merry Andrew" was the cleverest of these impostors. Pretending to be a relation from the country, he would speak, with tears in his eyes, of the fine qualities of the dear departed, and promise to return later with a coffin and a cart to remove the body to the family burial place. Sometimes he even sank so low as to bring with him "Praying Howard," who in a black suit and white choker, would impersonate a clergyman, and deliver a suitable address to the assembled "mourners."

This then was the situation when Dr Knox, in his turn as head of a School of Anatomy, had to search for "subjects." The market, although admittedly a very black market, was already there; it was for him to come to terms with it. Knox never hesitated. He was now a successful man, who never grudged money spent to further his art, so he decided quite simply to outbid his rivals. He made indeed the boast—which would have been better left unmade—that he could "always command 'subjects'." Later his enemies were to explain this by saying "he had the West Port villains in pay," but of course Knox only meant that he was prepared to pay the maximum price. In one year, as we know, he was reputed to have spent over £700 to ensure that his dissecting-rooms were never bare, and on one occasion, according to Lonsdale, he "actually paid 25 guineas rather than see his class disappointed," *i.e.*, more than double the normal charge for a "subject." He was in touch with the Resurrectionists of Dublin and London, and both there and at home he got the reputation of being a good, reliable employer who paid cash on delivery: "Knox is honourable in all his transactions" said an Irish agent, "Knox's word once passed I have never known him to violate." In fact one of the most impudent deeds ever to be accomplished by the Edinburgh Resurrection men was when they actually stole a corpse from the table in Lizars' dissecting-room and took it to Dr Knox.

It would be as well at this point to consider the nocturnal set-up at Surgeons' Square—the time when the Resurrection men made their deliveries. Dr Knox himself was rarely at No. 10 during the night, but seven students (the three seniors being Thomas Wharton Jones, William Fergusson, and Alexander Miller) worked on a rota system, with a porter, David Paterson, on duty all night. This man, who afterwards tried to push himself into the limelight, had only recently entered Dr Knox's service and although at the trial he claimed to be "keeper of the museum," he was no more than a porter, earning a wage of 7s. a week, and he was not above trying to do a dishonest deal with the Resurrectionists. However his duties, as far as his employer was concerned, were—apart from the daily cleaning of the rooms —"keeping the door . . . likewise to go messages, and be ready at all times to receive packages, and go for them." He took down the names of the men who brought the "packages"—they hardly ever, as has been shown, used their own—and the date of the reception of the bodies. He said that he had positive orders from the doctor not to interfere at all with these men, and much has been made of this statement in proof of Knox's guilt, but it surely can also be accepted as a quite necessary precaution: if too much curiosity had been shown in their affairs then these anonymous Resurrection men, some possibly responsible for other crimes, would have been quickly off to a rival firm. (In London, although apparently more rarely in Edinburgh, they played the most abominable tricks on any doctor who remonstrated with them, such as placing a decomposing body on his door-step, or informing the police where a stolen body could be found.)

Once the "package" was inside the house, the students noted "age, sex and general applicability to the wants of the class," and if suitable, accepted it and made the payment, the average price at this time being about £10 in winter, £8 in summer. The body was then consigned to a cold, damp cellar, and the next day placed on the dissecting-room table.

In this Dr Knox was simply following the usage of the day. He was using the normal channels for his supply of "subjects," the methods then employed by every surgeon in Great Britain, on both sides of the Border. He had put most responsible students in charge of his rooms; William Fergusson, who was later to become Sir William Fergusson, Bart., F.R.S., Serjeant-Surgeon to the Queen and President of the Royal College of Surgeons of England, and Thomas Wharton Jones, later Professor Wharton Jones of University College, London. He must have believed that everything was in order, and to suggest, as his enemies suggested, that after his heavy days in the Museum and lecture-theatre he should also have been on night duty, is manifestly absurd.

As Lord Cockburn was to say later:

> All our anatomists incurred a most unjust, and a very alarming, though not unnatural odium; Dr Knox in particular, against whom not only the anger of the populace, but the condemnation of more intelligent persons, was specially directed. But tried in reference to the invariable and the necessary practice of the profession, our anatomists were spotlessly correct, and Knox the most correct of them all.

The anatomists in London were at the same time employing precisely the same methods, and many were in much closer touch with the Resurrection men than ever Dr Knox had been. Sir Astley Cooper, the famous London surgeon, on whom no breath of scandal fell, thought nothing of supporting the wives and families of his purveyors of bodies, should they have the misfortune to find themselves in jail, and of indemnifying them for the time spent there. It was quite the recognised thing to do, as these accounts testify:

> Jan. 29 1828. Paid Mr Cock to pay Mr South half the expenses of bailing Vaughan from Yarmouth and going down. £14-7-0. 1829 6 May.

Paid Vaughan's wife 6/-. Paid Vaughan for 26 weeks' confinement at 10/- a week, £13-0-0.

But Sir Astley Cooper had the good fortune never to encounter murderers.

On 29 November 1827 fate had prepared for Robert Knox that sort of blow which, in a split second, can alter a man's whole life. On that day one of Dr Knox's students met in the University precincts two men who were looking for the Anatomy Rooms, but the zealous youth, on learning their errand, directed them to Dr Knox, 10 Surgeons' Square. There at nightfall they delivered in a sack the dead body of an old man, for which they received £7 10s. Had they not met that student, and had they carried their burden to Professor Monro, as had been their intention, and had he become their client, all the obloquy that was heaped on Knox might well have fallen instead upon Monro. The two men with the sack were Burke and Hare.

On that day, writes Dr Moores Ball:

> Robert Knox—a great, strong, outstanding and valiant character; the most eloquent, the most versatile, and the most thorough teacher of anatomy that Scotland, a country which long has been noted for the excellence of its anatomical instruction, ever has produced: Robert Knox—he who was designated as "Knox, primus et incomparabilis," had his life wrecked, ruined, and embittered by the fortuitous circumstances which caused the murderers, Burke and Hare, to cross his path.

As Knox himself said, although in a different context:

> Chance, which rules all living things, uncontrollable chance, setting at defiance all human calculations.[39]

6

All went well for about a year. Burke and Hare, on their own testimony, brought sixteen bodies to 10 Surgeons' Square, a small proportion—only about one-sixth—of the total employed, so that their visits were hardly noteworthy. Their names were entered in the porter's book, along with the others, as "John and

[39] *Lancet*, 11 Nov. 1854.

William"; they were no more suspicious characters than the rest of the evil gang. But as time went on, success bred in them such a swaggering bravado that they would risk delivering a box in day-light, its contents still warm; and they were so plausible that they easily deflected the questions put to them by the younger and much more innocent student receptionists.

They had, they explained, when they obtained possession of the bodies of those friendless souls who had died in the lodging houses of the Old Town, to remove them with the utmost speed —a matter, really, of common hygiene, as anyone who knew the cramped and crowded conditions of the lodging-houses would confirm. Conditions in the Old Town of Edinburgh in the early nineteenth century were worse even than in Naples, and the Scottish Poor Law Administration—or rather lack of it until 1845—permitted more destitution in Scotland than in the majority of European countries.

Burke's "open manner and ready excuse when boldly taken to task, told immeasurably in favour of the accuracy of his statement." It even got him round the awkward corner when William Fergusson (Knox's senior student) recognised the body of Mary Paterson, whom he had seen in the Canongate only a few nights previously. Mary Paterson was a woman of the town —an exceptionally beautiful girl of eighteen, who once seen, could not easily be forgotten, and Fergusson sought for an explanation of her sudden death and insisted on confronting Burke on his next visit in the presence of two gentlemen:

> Burke declared that he bought the corpse from an old hag in the Canongate, and that Paterson had killed herself with drink. He offered to go and show the house if they doubted him. His explanation was feasible; it rested on the whisky tendency of all such women—and Paterson's body smelt of liquor when brought in.

Fergusson did not pursue the matter further.

We have it on the authority of Lord Cockburn that William Burke, "except that he murdered," was "a sensible and what might be called a respectable man; not at all ferocious in his general manner." Burke was an Irishman, aged thirty-six, and he had apparently all the Irish gift of blarney, and when he chose, a certain amount of Irish charm. "Christopher North" (Professor John Wilson) described him as:

> A neat little man of about 5 ft. 5 in.—a very active but not a powerful man . . . not quarrelsome and a pleasant companion over a jug of toddy . . . nothing repulsive about him, and certainly not deficient in intelligence, his voice rather soft and calm.

Burke had come over from Ireland in 1818 to work as a labourer on the cutting of the Union Canal between Glasgow and Edinburgh. At Polmont, while on that task, he met Helen M'Dougal, "a woman of disreputable life," and together they went off to Peebles, Perth, Leith, and finally, in 1827, to Edinburgh, where they ultimately set up house on their own while Burke worked as a cobbler.

At first, on their arrival in Edinburgh, Burke and M'Dougal were paying guests in the lodging-house run by William Hare in Tanner's Close, a dirty lane opening off the West Port. This lodging-house was for the lowest and poorest type of traveller. It was a three-apartment house of one story, two of the rooms were large and contained eight beds, which were let at 3d. each, and sometimes as many as three persons slept in one bed; the third room was small, with one window looking out on to a dead wall and a pigsty. William Hare had, like Burke, come over from Ireland to work on the Union Canal (although the two men did not meet until 1827) and, when in Edinburgh, Hare lived in this tramps' lodging-house in Tanner's Close. It was then run by a man called Logue and his wife Margaret Laird—both Irish—and when Logue died in 1826 Hare came back to Edinburgh "to console the widow and succeed to the business." Hare was the same age as Burke, but otherwise they had little in common. In build Hare was heavier and more muscular than Burke, but "sluggish and inert," with a most unpleasant face, "at first look seemingly an idiot" reported Christopher North.

Of the women the same observer reports that they were:

> Poor, miserable, bony, skinny, scranky, wizened jades both, without the most distant approach to good-lookingness . . . peevish, sulky, savage and cruel and evidently familiar from earliest life with all the woe and wretchedness of guilt and pollution.

E
59

Of the two he thought that Mrs Hare "had most of the she-devil," and she was certainly a cleverer woman than Helen M'Dougal who "was of a dour and sullen disposition, morosely jealous and gloomily wicked."

These then were the protagonists of the drama which was about to open, for retribution came on 31 October 1828. On that day Burke offered free bed and breakfast to a Mrs Docherty, a frail old woman whom he had found begging in the streets that morning. She told him that she had come to the city from Ireland to look for her son, and he at once offered her hospitality, pretending to believe her to be a distant relative; although, to accommodate her, he had to move his lodgers, an ex-soldier, James Gray, and his wife and child, over to the Hares in Tanner's Close.

In the evening, it being the night of Hallowe'en, they all attended a neighbour's party, where there was drinking and singing and dancing; even Mrs Docherty danced, but next morning, when the Grays returned for their breakfast, there was no sign of her. They enquired for her, and Helen M'Dougal, "in foul terms replied that the visitor had been 'ow'r friendly' with Burke, and that she had in consequence kicked her out of the house." But Mrs Gray's curiosity was aroused; Burke was behaving in a peculiar manner—throwing whisky all over the place—and he seemed anxious to keep her away from a heap of straw at the foot of the bed. At last, but not until dusk, she and her husband found themselves alone in the room, and when she had pulled aside the straw Mrs Gray found beneath it the naked and blood-stained body of a dead woman, whom to their horror, they recognised as Mrs Docherty. Without a moment's hesitation, and refusing to be bribed by Helen M'Dougal whom they met on the way, the Grays went straight to the Police Station and returned with a police officer who, although the body meantime had been removed, got sufficient evidence to take Burke and M'Dougal into custody, and to arrest Mr and Mrs Hare twelve hours later.

The police found Mrs Docherty's body on the following day, Sunday, 2 November, when "on information received," they visited Dr Knox's rooms in Surgeons' Square at 7 a.m. There, in an unopened tea-chest, said by the porter to have been "brought to him the night before in the ordinary course of business," was the corpse of Mrs Docherty—a woman killed solely for the price which could be obtained for her dead body, a fact which the citizens of Edinburgh recognised with mounting horror.

Dr Knox at first appeared to take the matter fairly lightly. He had no reason, then, to believe that the body of Mrs Docherty was other than that of one of the many unclaimed strangers who died natural deaths in the city. Nor was it reasonable to suspect, with such a wealth of "subjects" ready to hand in the hovels and graveyards of Edinburgh, that Resurrection men, who had been doing a professional job for many years, should suddenly turn into murderers. Knox's dealings with Burke and Hare had been precisely similar to those which he and his colleagues had had over the years with such men as "Moudiewarp" and "Merry Andrew"; he himself had only twice spoken to Burke and Hare, and he had all along kept clear of personal contact with the Resurrectionists—his love for science had never led him, like Liston, to join them in the churchyards; he had dealt with them simply in the way of business. As the owner of a private anatomical school in Scotland he had no legal claim to any "subjects," and in any case the number of bodies which the law permitted to be dissected was but a fraction of the number required annually by British medical students. In London, where there were 800 medical students, there were in one year (1831) "only eleven bodies which could be legally disposed of as Subjects"; the number in Edinburgh would probably have been even less.

Dr Knox and his fellow anatomists were by no means blind to the risks they ran. Indeed, during the preceding years the teachers of anatomy all over Britain had been urging the Government to take action and introduce a Bill by which the bodies of all unknown persons without friends, who died in workhouses or hospitals, should be handed over to them, under proper controls, for use in the schools. Apart from the impossibility of obtaining a sufficient number of "subjects" by legal means (and in England only the bodies of murderers could be so used) the anatomists also pointed out how grossly unfair it was that:

> proper skill in practical anatomy was enforced by the Legislature upon every medical man, while the means of securing its pursuit rendered him liable to disgrace and punishment.

On 1 April 1828, *i.e., before* the discovery of the Burke and Hare murders, the Royal College of Surgeons of Edinburgh, of which Dr Knox was a Fellow, sent a Memorial to the Home Secretary, Sir Robert Peel, upon the subject. In it, after stressing the importance of the teaching of anatomy, and the difficulty, under the existing law, of doing so without committing criminal acts, the Surgeons pointed out that the ensuing scarcity of bodies for dissecting led not only to the demoralisation of those engaged in procuring them, but also involved both teachers and students in "oppressive" expense. Consequently students of medicine and surgery tended to go abroad, to the detriment of the British Schools. The Surgeons, therefore, commended the subject to the "serious consideration of the Legislature."

Some months later, during the very week-end when Burke and Hare were arrested, Dr Knox must have been penning an independent memorandum to Sir Robert Peel, because Creswell, the historian of the Royal College of Surgeons of Edinburgh, states that such a letter, bearing the date 3 November 1828, and which perhaps for obvious reasons was never despatched, is in the archives of the College. In this letter Knox concentrated on two of the obstacles he had encountered in the course of his work. In the first place he accused the Dublin anatomists of being obstructionists. In that city there was such an abundance of "subjects" that they were not in demand, and yet, presumably owing to professional jealousy, the Irish lecturers went to the length of procuring warrants, so that the "packages" addressed to Edinburgh might be broken open on the decks of the ships transporting them, and their contents left to rot on the quays in order to rouse popular indignation against Scottish anatomists. This, wrote Knox, had actually happened to one of his recent consignments. Even worse was the behaviour of the officers of H.M. Customs and Excise. Knox had "packages" opened by them at Liverpool, with much publicity, also at Greenock, where an exposure was made which alarmed the whole district. At Carlisle, with unnecessary zeal, these same officials removed a box from the northbound Edinburgh coach and caused a quite futile inquest to be held on the body they discovered inside. All this worried Knox very considerably. He continued:

> There is one subject in particular on which I beg most respectfully your attention. Anatomists generally are most anxious to avoid public scenes such as these, and for this purpose they are careful to select subjects which are claimed by no relative or friend, and thus often avoid the painful necessity of violating the burial grounds and by so doing inflicting a shock on the most sacred feelings of human nature. Now, when anatomical subjects procured under such circumstances are nevertheless seized on their way to the schools, very alarming reprisals are made in the burying grounds of the place where the seizure has been made, often without the smallest regard to risk or circumstances.

In his last paragraph Knox again emphasised his belief in the importance of giving to an uninstructed public as little information as possible about the running of the anatomical schools. Silence on this important point was later to cost him dear, but he believed it to be in the interests of science. In this undelivered letter to the Home Secretary, he also wrote:

> Permit me most respectfully to remark to you, that I have ever been an advocate for the making of these matters as little public as possible, but now that the anatomical enquiry is patent to all, I therefore thought it my duty to state to you the obstacles which impede the progress of anatomy in Great Britain.[40]

The anatomists had indeed pushed their point so far that Sir Robert Peel, who was sympathetic to their cause, had set up a Select Committee under the Chairmanship of Mr Henry Warburton, to investigate the whole subject. The Committee spent two very busy months examining witnesses, and in July 1828, their Report was published, their terms of reference having been "to enquire into the manner of obtaining subjects for Dissection in the Schools of Anatomy, and into the State of the

[40] C. H. Creswell, *Royal College of Surgeons of Edinburgh*, Edinburgh and London. 1926.

Law affecting the Persons employed in dissecting Bodies." Their conclusions were favourable to the anatomists:

> To neglect the practice of dissection would lead to the greatest aggravation of human misery; since Anatomy, if not learned by that practice, must be learned by mangling the living.

But still the Government took no action.

Dr Knox hoped that now good would come out of evil, and that the Burke and Hare scandal would force the Government to bring this Report out of the pigeon-hole where it had been nestling for nearly six months and introduce some effective legislation. As for himself, he thought that "the matter would subside in a short period"; this was a great and fundamental error, but at first he seemed unable to believe that murder had been committed, still less that any reasonable person could suspect him of being a party to it.

His medical brethren were the first to disillusion him. To Dr Knox it must have seemed a stroke of sheer bad luck that, of all the anatomists in Edinburgh, Burke and Hare should have chanced upon him; he expected that the more fortunate majority of the surgeons would adopt the line, "There, but for the grace of God, go I"; but their attitude was, on the contrary, "holier than thou." It was a stab in the back which Knox never forgot nor forgave; in future he castigated his colleagues without mercy, later he was to say bitterly "better to have no friends than doubtful ones."

At the beginning it never seemed to occur to Dr Knox that he could be linked, even in the public mind, with the criminals, Burke and Hare; but public opinion, already overexcited by the activities of the grave-robbers, was roused to frenzy at the thought of murder. Dr Knox was an anatomist: Dr Knox had employed Burke and Hare to bring him bodies, and that was enough. The people refused to believe that he had not known that he was dealing with murderers. It was soon brought home to Dr Knox that the citizens of Edinburgh regarded him in an even worse light than Burke and Hare, as he was generally held to be not only their partner, but their patron and the instigator of their crimes, possibly even their instructor in the art of "burking."

64

These sentiments were further stimulated by broadsides and news-sheets relating the gruesome details of the murders. Popular ballads also appeared daily, of which one of the most quotable and least offensive is:

> Up the close and doon the stair
> Ben the hoose wi' Burke and Hare,
> Burke's the butcher, Hare's the thief,
> Knox the boy who buys the beef.

One news-sheet was actually headed with a portrait of Knox above a poem "A Timely Hint to Anatomical Practitioners" which contained the following lines:

> Men, women, children, old and young,
>   The sickly and the hale,
> Were murdered, packed up, and sent off
>   To K——'s human sale.
>
> That man of skill, with subjects warm,
>   Was frequently supplied,
> Nor did he question when or how
>   The person brought had died.

Artists produced topical lithographs: "Wretch's Illustrations of Shakespeare," and "Noxiana," "Cropping a Nox-i-ous Plant," etc. Even children were scared into good behaviour—or else "Burke and Hare would get them," and at their play they sang rhymes like:

> Burke an' Hare
> Fell doun the stair,
> Wi' a body in a box
> Gaun to Doctor Knox.

Doctor Knox was certainly left in no doubt that the populace considered him to be a murderer, and worse, a villain of the deepest dye. But there was nothing he could well do about it, as more than six weeks were to elapse before the trial could take place, owing to the extraordinary legal tangle into which the lawyers had been thrown by such an unprecedented affair.

7

In accordance with the practice of Scots Law, the Sheriff had immediately, on 3 November, interrogated his four prisoners, Mr and Mrs Hare, William Burke, and Helen M'Dougal, and got from them entirely contradictory statements; in fact each one told a bigger and better lie about the manner in which Mrs Docherty had met her death, and all denied having had any part in it. This was confusing enough, but the Public Prosecutor was confronted by an even greater problem: the provision of proof that in the case of Mrs Docherty murder had actually been committed.

Today, when medical reports can be relied upon for information as to the precise time, before or after death, at which bruises have been inflicted on a corpse, it is easy to condemn Dr Knox for failure to recognise such visible proofs of crime on the bodies sold to him. What must be remembered is that in 1828 neither Dr Knox nor any other doctor had been trained to distinguish between ante- and post-mortem conditions. Also the method of "burking," *i.e.*, smothering, left no marks on neck or face.

Not until the question was raised by this very murder was any research done on the subject, when the first investigations were made by a witness at the trial, Dr Christison (later Sir Robert Christison, Professor of Medical Jurisprudence at Edinburgh) who wrote:

> There was no information in books worth using on the effects of injuries inflicted immediately after death, while the blood is fluid and the body warm. It turned out that the marks left in that case approached much nearer to those from injuries inflicted during life; that they are a source of dangerous fallacy, but that they may be distinguished by sufficient characters in careful hands. My attention was specially drawn to the effects of blows and dislocations immediately after death by the appearances I observed in the dead body of a woman murdered by the notorious body-snatchers Burke and Hare.

It is not therefore surprising—the method of "burking" being then unsuspected—that the police surgeon, Mr Alexander Black, who first saw the body of Mrs Docherty on 2 November, refused to give a statement on the cause of death. His private opinion was that she had died of violence, but "medically," he said, he could give no opinion "quite certain, of the cause of death." At the trial he explained that he had seen many bodies with similar symptoms produced by suffocation, through drinking, the intoxicated person having fallen face downwards on one of the puddles so frequently found on the streets of Edinburgh. He made the point clearly under cross-examination by Henry Cockburn:

"Have you ever seen a case of suffocation separate from strangling?"
"I have known many cases of drink, of people lying on the street, brought in in that way."
"Were the appearances the same?"
"Very similar as in this old woman."
"Have you had much experience in cases of persons that you knew were suffocated?"
"I can't say that, except from drink."
"What do you mean when you talk of cases coming in to the Police Office as cases of suffocation: were they all from drink?"
"Yes, I have known six cases in one night. It was in November last, and we did not know which to apply to first."
"From drinking?"
"From drinking."

Even Christison, who did an autopsy on Mrs Docherty on 2 and 3 November would hazard nothing more precise than "death by violence is very probable. I do not think that the medical circumstances could justify a more certain opinion."

It was an interesting case, for the dead body was that of a woman "without a trace of disease in any organ and well nourished" and although it showed signs of asphyxia, there were no external marks to prove it. In his autobiography Christison recorded the puzzling facts:

We found indeed, various immaterial bruises on the limbs. . . . But there were no external marks about the neck or face to indicate how respiration had been obstructed. . . . At this time we knew nothing of the supposed manner of death, and therefore a question arose whether death might not have been occasioned by the head having been forcibly bent upon the breast so as to rupture the spinal ligaments. Express trial, however, proved that such forcible flexure, practised very soon after death . . . produced the same appearances of extravasation as in the body we had examined. . . . We therefore came to the conclusion that the injury to the cervical spine

67

had been caused soon after death . . . that if death by violence were to be assumed, smothering and not strangling was the manner of it; but that there was no positive proof of death in that way, or indeed in what way death had been caused.

Dr Knox was not alone in not recognising murder at first sight.

When the month of November had drawn to a close and the doctors could produce no proofs of the murder and the prisoners still refused to admit any share in it, the Lord Advocate, Sir William Rae, became impatient. Hare and his wife had been twice re-examined, on 10 and 19 November, and on both occasions had "denied all accession to the murder, and stated that Docherty had not received any violence from any person in their presence." Burke, at his second examination, declared that Mrs Docherty had crawled, in a state of intoxication, into the straw where she was found, and had suffocated there, that no violence had been done to the old woman in life, but that "a good deal of force was necessary to get the body into the chest, as it was stiff." Craftily, or more probably merely by chance, Burke had brought the problem full circle—back to the thorny question of post-mortem bruising.

It was obvious that the case for the Crown was getting nowhere, and a trial, with so little available evidence, and in which the fact of a murder having been committed was not "beyond the possibility of question," might well end in acquittal. Now this was the last thing the Lord Advocate wanted to happen, as he had reason to believe that other crimes of a similar nature had been committed, and he was most anxious to ascertain if the prisoners were part of a larger group. So, after mature deliberation, Sir William Rae decided that one of the four should be induced to turn King's evidence: Helen M'Dougal resolutely refused to say anything, Burke was manifestly the master-mind who should be made to stand his trial, Mrs Hare could not be condemned on her husband's evidence, and so the choice fell on Hare. Hare, despicable rascal that he was, required little encouragement to confess. On 1 December, having received an assurance from the Procurator-Fiscal that "if he would disclose the facts relative to the case of Docherty, and to such other crimes of a similar nature, committed by Burke, of which he was cognisant, he should not be brought to trial on account of his accession to any of these crimes," he made a full confession.

Unfortunately his confession has completely disappeared. William Roughead made an exhaustive search for it in the archives of the Justiciary Office when he was writing his book on Burke and Hare in the "Notable British Trials Series," but all to no avail. Contemporary evidence, however, disclosed that Hare's confession tallied fairly well with the extant confessions made by Burke after the trial, and the Lord Advocate expressly stated that:

> Hare emitted a declaration, detailing the circumstances connected with the murder of Mary Docherty, and with similar crimes in which Burke had been engaged. Of these the murder of James Wilson and of Mary Paterson were two; and it was from the facts which Hare so detailed, that evidence was obtained from unexceptionable witnesses of such a nature as enabled those two murders to be brought forward as substantive acts, in the same indictment which charged Burke with the murder of Mary Docherty.

The whole sorry, sordid story had now come to light. Burke and Hare were no Resurrection men; they had no stomach for the alarums and excursions of churchyard work—now become more difficult than ever owing to the ruses of the relatives, who were erecting watch-houses, covering the graves with iron cages, and burying the dead in cast-iron coffins. These two scoundrels had fallen into the way of providing "subjects" for Dr Knox purely by chance; the body which they first brought to Surgeons' Square on the night of 29 November 1827 was that of a man who had died a natural death in his bed—but that bed was one of those in Hare's Lodging-house in Tanner's Close at the West Port. This old man was an army pensioner, named Donald, who had the misfortune to die a few weeks before he had drawn his usual quarterly allowance—thus leaving his landlord, Hare, with a bad debt of £4. It was to recoup himself for this that Hare suddenly had the brilliant idea of selling the body "to the doctors," and in order to do this he enlisted the aid of his lodger, Burke, who had no scruples in agreeing to help him.

Burke very sensibly pointed out that they would at least have to wait until the arrival—and departure—of the undertaker.

However, when he had come and gone, Hare chiselled up the lid of the coffin, removed the old man's body, and hid it in a bed, filling up the coffin with tanner's bark from the yard outside; later they respectfully watched it being taken away for burial, after which, having, as we know, interviewed the student in the University Quadrangle, they carried the body in a sack to 10 Surgeons' Square. There, Burke says, they were received by three students, but Dr Knox then came in "and looked at the body, and proposed they should get £7 10s, and he asked no questions as to how the body had been obtained." Hare and Burke thereupon divided the spoils, £4 5s to Hare and £3 5s to Burke, and the students wished them a very good-night, saying "that they would be glad to see them again when they had any other body to dispose of."

It can be imagined that Burke and Hare went home in high good humour with their easily won wealth. It augured a successful future for them, but they did not yet contemplate ensuring it by murder, although they may have pleasurably observed the old and frail among the lodgers at Tanner's Close. At any rate they seem to have taken no active steps until some time in the following February, when one of Hare's lodgers, Joseph the miller, fell ill with what the neighbours believed to be fever. This worried Mr and Mrs Hare "in case it should keep away lodgers" and so, with this double incentive, Burke and Hare decided to expedite the work of nature; as Joseph was a dying man in any case, and too weak to put up any sort of resistance, they quickly smothered him by putting a pillow over his face. Again they took the body to Surgeons' Square, and this time received £10 for it. (Of this sum Hare took £6 and Burke £4. Although Hare may have looked mentally deficient and although Burke was undoubtedly a man of higher intelligence, Burke certainly always got the worst of the financial bargain; every time Mrs Hare insisted on getting a rake-off of £1.)

It was all too easy: Burke and Hare were now launched on their criminal career, and developed for their purpose the special technique which became known as "burking." They first tried it out on a sick match-seller, an Englishman, who was also lodging with Hare; they "got above him and held him down, and by holding his mouth suffocated him, and disposed of him in the same manner." This method left no marks of violence on the body—no wonder the doctors had been mystified by the manner of Mrs Docherty's death. It was the method used by the two villains for all their subsequent murders. They soon got tired of waiting for ailing lodgers, and did as they were to do to Mrs Docherty. They lured people in from the streets, made them incapably drunk, and then took them into the little back room looking on to the pigsty—and then to Dr Knox's.

On 11 February 1828 a poor old beggar woman, Abigail Simpson, was done to death after having been plied with liquor until she was unconscious. "Hare clapped his hand on her mouth and nose and Burke laid himself across her body." Next day, having reported at Surgeons' Square, a porter met them in the evening at the back of the Castle and helped them to convey the body in a tea-chest to No. 10. Here, for the second and last time, they met Dr Knox who "approved of the body being so fresh, but did not ask any questions," and again they received £10.

With horrible regularity and uniformity the murders continued. As Christopher North said: "First ae drunk auld wife, and then anither drunk auld wife, and then a third drunk auld wife, and then a drunk auld sick man or twa," They were:

1. An old cinder gatherer, named Effie, who was in the habit of selling to Burke the scraps of leather she came across in the course of her trade.
2. An unknown woman whom Burke saw drunk and incapable in the hands of the police, who handed her over to him when he kindly offered to take her home, saying he "knew where she lodged." Burke at this time, it should be observed, had "a good character with the police."
3. and 4. Two unnamed women who were decoyed into the house and killed, one by Burke, the other by Hare.
5. Another woman killed by Hare during Burke's absence in the country. This led to a quarrel between the partners—as Hare had not shared out with Burke the £8 he had received and was probably the cause of Burke and M'Dougal ceasing

71

to be Hare's lodgers and removing to a basement room in a house nearer to the West Port.

6. Ann M'Dougal, actually a relative of Helen M'Dougal, whom she had invited to come from Falkirk to visit her.

7. A washer-woman named Mrs Hostler.

8. and 9. Mary Haldane, a woman of the streets—"a stout old woman, with but one tooth in her mouth" who had once been a lodger with Hare. After a few days her daughter, Peggy, who followed her mother's profession, began to make enquiries for her, and called at the lodging-house in Tanner's Close. She was invited by Hare to come inside, told circumstantially that her mother had left to go to Mid-Calder, and further invited to share Burke's bottle of whisky. Thereafter she joined her mother in Dr Knox's cellar.

10. and 11. The most callous crime that Burke and Hare perhaps ever committed was in the month of June 1828, when they murdered an old woman and her grandson, a dumb and feeble-minded boy of about twelve, who had come from Glasgow and were lodging with Hare. "At the dead hour of night" they suffocated the grandmother in her bed and fell on the boy as he sat by the fire in the kitchen.

Burke was always haunted by the appealing look in this boy's eyes, and certainly he showed a little more remorse for his crimes than Hare, who was quite without conscience. Hare, unlike Macbeth, never lost a night's sleep, whereas Burke, according to his own confession:

> could not sleep without a bottle of whisky by his bed-side, and a two-penny candle to burn all night beside him; when he awoke he would take a draught of the bottle—sometimes half-a-bottle at a draught—and that would make him sleep.

Both men were usually in a high state of intoxication when they committed the murders.

These eleven murders, plus Docherty, Joseph the miller, and the match-seller, are all mentioned in Burke's confession, and presumably in Hare's, but except in the case of Docherty, where the police had found the body, there was no real evidence of any of them. Some people, indeed, thought that not so many persons had in actual fact been done away with, and that the murderers (Burke having said that they might as well be hung for a sheep as a lamb) were glorying in their guilt, and even magnifying their crimes. Others believed that sixteen was a low estimate of the number of murders committed by the two partners "singly or together." Of that the law could have no cognisance, but there were those other two murders revealed in Hare's confession, that of Mary Paterson (the girl whom Fergusson had recognised in Knox's rooms) and that of "Daft Jamie," a well-known Edinburgh "character," when Burke and Hare had sadly overreached themselves and left evidence and witnesses for the police to find and produce.

Mary Paterson, although she had no relatives in Edinburgh, had been in the company of a friend, Janet Brown, when on the ill-omened morning of 9 April 1828, she met Burke in a public house. Burke treated the two girls to three gills of rum and bitters, and then invited them to breakfast "at his lodgings." Here he varied the usual pattern of his crime: he led the girls not to Tanner's Close, but to his brother's house in Gibb's Close in the Canongate, where he gave them tea, bread, eggs, Finnan haddocks, and more whisky. Mary Paterson was soon dead drunk and sound asleep, and even the storming temper of Helen M'Dougal, who came in and discovered the festive party, failed to rouse her. But it frightened Janet Brown so much that she, who in some extraordinary fashion had succeeded in remaining sober, insisted on leaving the house at once. She returned to lodgings where she and Mary Paterson had once stayed, and told their friend, the owner, Mrs Lawrie, what had happened. Mrs Lawrie, who was to act as this silly girl's guardian angel, immediately sent her back, accompanied by a servant, to fetch Mary. They could not at first locate the house, and when they ultimately found it they were received by Mr and Mrs Hare who told them that Burke and Mary had gone out together but would soon be back, and invited Janet to come in and have another drink while she waited for them; she accepted the invitation and sent the maid home. Fortunately for Janet, who otherwise would undoubtedly have become the seventeenth victim, Mrs Lawrie sent the girl back forthwith, with strict orders that Janet should instantly return, and this she did as the Hares now feared Mrs Lawrie and made no effort to detain her. In the afternoon Janet went back yet again, and by herself, to enquire for Mary; this time she met Burke's sister-in-law who told her that he and Mary had not yet returned. Although Janet and a Mrs Worthington, the owner of the lodging-house which Mary had quitted so precipitately on 9 April, continued to make discreet enquiries (without, of course, going to the police) they could find no trace of their missing friend.

The delay of some twenty minutes which had occurred when Janet and the maid were looking for the house in Gibb's Close had been fatal for Mary Paterson. Burke had sent his sister-in-law out to fetch Hare, and within a few minutes the two ruffians had dealt with the insensible girl "in the usual manner." The dead body of her companion must have been hidden in the bed close beside her, when Janet Brown accepted that second drink from the Hares. Within four hours it had been delivered at Dr Knox's, and payment received.

Had Dr Knox's student, William Fergusson, who recognised Mary Paterson, insisted upon pursuing his enquiries, murder would have been out in April 1828 instead of in November. As it was Burke had effectively lulled all suspicion at Surgeons' Square. Dr Knox's first action on seeing the corpse was hardly that of a guilty man in possession of the body of a murdered girl:

> he brought a Mr—, a painter, to look at her, she was so handsome a figure, and well shaped in body and limbs.

This was typical of Knox, who believed that abstract beauty must be combined with form, without which there can be no real beauty. "Absolute beauty," he wrote later, "resides alone in the fully developed form of woman, as represented by the antique sculptors."[41] Many of the art students who frequented the rooms also made drawings of Mary Paterson, after the manner of the Rokeby Venus.

All this, surely, would never have been permitted by a man with anything to conceal. Dr Knox, moreover, was in no hurry to dissect the body, which owing to its perfection of muscular form,

[41] *Fau's Anatomy of the External Forms of Man*, London 1849, p. 263.

PLATE 4

Photograph of Dr Knox.
By courtesy of the Royal College of Surgeons
of Edinburgh

he retained to illustrate his lectures on the muscles in the later part of his course—giving it thus a two-fold publicity.

The other victim to be killed with utter recklessness by Burke and Hare was James Wilson, "Daft Jamie." Daft Jamie was a good-natured, feeble-minded lad of eighteen, who in the contemporary drawings, looks as though he might have been a spastic, although he must have had considerable physical strength. He lived a vagrant's life in the Old Town of Edinburgh, earning a small livelihood by doing light casual work.

Of all the sixteen murders none struck the public imagination so forcibly, nor roused public indignation so violently, as did this of Daft Jamie when the details became known.

> He's to be pitied, that's such a silly elf,
> Who cannot speak nor wrestle for himself.
> Jamie was such a simpleton
> He'd not fight with a boy.
> Nor did he ever curse or swear
> At those who'd him annoy.

This was typical of the hundreds of verses which found their way into print in chap-books and broadsides. Another example is an "elegiac" poem of sixteen verses beginning:

> Attendance give, whilst I relate
> How Poor Daft Jamie met his fate.
> 'Twill make your hair stand on your head [heid]
> As I unfold the horrid deed.

According to Burke, Poor Daft Jamie was lured to his death by Mrs Hare, who enticed him into her house and offered him a dram. Jamie, however, was an abstemious boy, and they could only persuade him to drink one glass of whisky. In consequence, when Burke and Hare set about him they were confronted for the first time with a young man, albeit mentally deficient, who was neither drunk nor altogether a weakling: "he made a terrible resistance" reports Burke, "Hare and him fell off the bed and struggled." But with Burke ready to grip his hands and feet, the boy never had a chance. He was murdered at midday on one October morning of 1828, and in the evening was taken to Dr Knox's.

At Dr Knox's this body seems to have aroused no suspicions at all, and was not recognised although it was laid out for dissection in the ordinary way. The only suggestion that anything was amiss came later from David Paterson, Dr Knox's door-keeper, who is supposed to be the anonymous author (the self-styled "Echo of Surgeons' Square") of an open "Letter to the Lord Advocate Disclosing the Accomplices, Secrets and Other Facts Relative to the Late Murders; with a Correct Account of the Manner in which the Anatomical Schools are supplied with subjects," a publication (8vo, 36 pp.) which sold for 6d. at No. 132 High Street, Edinburgh, but not until the New Year of 1829.

In this "Letter" Dr Knox was accused of "all along persisting that was not Jamie" and of ordering an immediate dissection of the body when the news got out that Daft Jamie was missing. But for us with the gift of hindsight, no witness appears quite so unreliable as this David Paterson on whose sole word this evidence rests. David Paterson at the trial declared that he was the "keeper of Dr Knox's museum" although, as the students were quick to point out, he was no more than the porter who attended to the dissecting-rooms. Nevertheless he succeeded at the trial in having himself addressed by Lord Meadowbank as "a medical person." At the time he seems to have imposed upon everyone; it was only after he had sent a rather ill-advised contribution to the *Caledonian Mercury* that the truth came out. In the first place he had been a disloyal servant to his master, for there was proof that he had been bargaining with other lecturers to organise sales to them on a commission basis of bodies brought to him for Dr Knox. Also it was generally believed that he had been on the point of going to Ireland with Burke, to act as his partner as a collector of "subjects" to send home to Hare.

Undismayed by these revelations, Paterson wrote three months later to Sir Walter Scott, offering him a "collection of anecdotes" of Surgeons' Square. Little as Sir Walter by then liked Knox (obviously believing him to be Burke's accomplice) he liked Paterson less; in his *Journal* for 4 April 1829 he wrote:

> I have a letter from one David Paterson, who was Dr Knox's jackall for bringing murdered bodies,—suggesting that I should write on the subject of Burke and Hare, and offering me his invaluable collection of

anecdotes. . . . "Did you ever hear the like?" The scoundrel has been the companion and patron of such atrocious murderers and kidnappers, and he has the impudence to write to any decent man.

So much for Dr Knox's porter David Paterson. Fortunately the Lord Advocate could provide better witnesses as Hare's confession had provided a rich harvest and the case for the Crown now seemed secure. No jury could fail to convict on the evidence to be put before it: in all three cases the police had found in Burke's possession some of the clothes of the victims "a black waist-coat, a dark printed cotton gown, a red-striped bed-gown," etc. and also the brass snuff-box and rather unusual snuff spoon belonging to Daft Jamie. In Mary Paterson's case, Janet Brown, who could identify Burke would be a most useful witness. Here at last was murder "without possibility of question."

Thus armed the Crown drew up its case, and on 8 December 1828 the prisoners, William Burke and Helen M'Dougal were served with their indictment for the murders of Mary Paterson, Daft Jamie, and Mrs Docherty. With that disregard which early nineteenth-century Presbyterian Scotland had for Christmas either as a holiday or a holy day the date of the trial was fixed for 24 December, Christmas Eve.

8

Excitement ran high in Edinburgh on that Christmas Eve of 1828; as tremendous public interest had been aroused in this "new and unparalleled crime." That those in authority expected disturbances is clear, for military forces—the infantry at the Castle and the cavalry at Piershill—were kept at the ready. However nothing untoward occurred when the prisoners were brought from the Calton Jail to the Justiciary Court-house in Parliament Close, although the approaches to it had been crowded since dawn. The doors of the Court-house were opened at 9 a.m. and instantly "every available inch of space was crowded to suffocation"; half an hour later the prisoners William Burke and Helen M'Dougal were placed at the bar. Burke wore a shabby blue surtout buttoned close to the throat, and looked far from ferocious. M'Dougal was "miserably dressed" in a small gray-coloured velvet bonnet, very much the worse for wear, a printed cotton shawl and cotton gown. The *Courant* reported that:

> Burke's features appeared to be firm and determined, yet in his haggard and wandering eye, there was at times a deep expression of trouble, as he unconsciously surveyed the preparations which were going forward.
>
> The female prisoner appeared to be more disturbed; every now and then her breast heaved with a deep drawn sigh, and her looks were desponding.

Both prisoners pled "Not Guilty."

The Court met at 10 a.m. The Presiding Judge was the Lord Justice-Clerk, the Rt. Hon David Boyle, and with him were Lords Pitmilly, Meadowbank, and Mackenzie; the Counsel for the Crown were the Lord Advocate, Sir William Rae, Bart., and three Advocates-Depute. The Counsel for the accused were, for Burke: Sir James W. Moncrieff (Dean of Faculty), Patrick Robertson, Duncan M'Neill and David Milne; for M'Dougal: Henry Cockburn (later Lord Cockburn), Mark Napier, Hugh Napier, Hugh Bruce, and George Patton. Fifty-five witnesses had also been called, of whom Dr Knox and his three students made up Nos. 44, 46, 47, and 48.

Referring to the defendants' Counsel, Roughead states that:

> It is a remarkable tribute to the evenhandedness of Scots justice that so brilliant a bar was found gratuitously to represent such "Poor" clients, though no doubt the high importance of the case, and the universal interest which it evoked were sufficient to compensate these gentlemen for any pecuniary loss.

They were, at any rate, determined to do their best; as soon as the case opened they initiated an extensive argument about "relevancy." M'Neill, for Burke, submitted that he was not bound to plead to, or to be tried upon, an indictment

> which not only charges him with three unconnected murders, committed each at a different time, and at a different place, but also combines his trial with that of another (M'Dougal) who is not even alleged to have had concern with two of the offences of which he is accused.

As for Helen M'Dougal:

> She is accused of one murder, committed in October 1828, and of no other offence. Yet she is placed on an indictment along with a different person,

who is accused of other two murders, each of them committed at a different time and at a different place,—it not being alleged that she had any connection with either of these crimes.

Mr Robertson then rose in support of these "defences" and promised to put before the Court, as shortly as he could, the reasons why the trial "upon this indictment should not be allowed to proceed." He then launched into an extremely lengthy discourse to which the Lord Advocate replied. He was in his turn answered by the Dean of Faculty (Sir James Moncrieff) followed by Lords Pitmilly, Meadowbank, and Mackenzie. At long last the legal wrangle ended, and the defendants' Counsel found themselves successful, the decision being that:

> in the circumstances of this case, and in consequence of the motion of the [defendants'] Counsel, the charges ought to be separately proceeded in; and that the Lord Advocate is entitled to select which charge shall be first brought to trial.

This put the Lord Advocate in something of a quandary, as he now had to decide which one, and one only, of the three charges he should choose for the trial of the prisoners. That he finally decided on the Docherty case, instead of that of Mary Paterson, or Daft Jamie, may have been due to the consideration, that not only was it the most recent of the crimes, but that in this case, and in this case alone, it had been possible to produce a body. Whatever his reasons, the Lord Advocate declared that he would proceed with the trial of Burke on the third charge of the indictment (the murder of Mrs Docherty) in which Helen M'Dougal was "art and part" guilty along with Burke.

Now this may not have changed the course of justice, but it did make an enormous difference to the position of Dr Knox. By thus reducing the number of the charges to one, the prisoners were being tried for the murder of the one person out of the whole sixteen whose body Dr Knox and his students had never seen— the police having discovered it at Surgeons' Square in a still unopened tea-chest. In consequence of this the Surgeons' Square team, witnesses Nos. 44, 46, 47 and 48—Dr Knox, Wharton Jones, Fergusson, and Miller—were never called upon to give evidence.

Once the question of "relevancy" had been settled, the trial could proceed. Witnesses who had seen Mrs Docherty meet Burke, and those who could testify to her previous good health, were examined, as were the neighbours who had attended the Hallowe'en party, and later had been kept awake by the noisy quarrelling of Burke and Hare, in the midst of which, testified the man who lived in the flat above, there had been other strangled cries, and a woman's voice had been heard screaming "Murder!" Mr and Mrs Gray, who had found the body, were questioned, as was the police officer who had accompanied them back to Burke's house after they had reported the murder at the police station. The porters also were examined, McCulloch who had carried the tea-chest to Dr Knox's and David Paterson who had received it. After that came the moment for which all the crowded Court had been impatiently waiting: the swearing-in of Mr and Mrs Hare as witnesses. Hare, who was evidently a very repulsive looking fellow, was sworn in by Lord Meadowbank, who afterwards explained to him the position in which he found himself by turning King's Evidence:

> We observe that you are at present a prisoner in the Tolbooth of Edinburgh, and from what we know, the Court understands that you must have had some concern in the transaction now under investigation. It is, therefore, my duty to inform you, that whatever share you might have had in that transaction, if you now speak the truth you can never afterwards be questioned in a court of justice.

Thus reassured, Hare had no hesitation in telling all; in fact the *Caledonian Mercury* reported that he "was disposed to be extremely communicative, and apparently had no idea that anything he had stated was at all remarkable or extraordinary."

His tale was that after the Hallowe'en party, when they were all drunk, including Mrs Docherty, he and Burke began to quarrel. Mrs Docherty, who was anxious to help Burke, ran twice out into the passage, crying "Murder" or "Police." She was fetched back by Helen M'Dougal, and in the general disorder was pushed over a little stool by Hare, and lay there, too drunk to rise. Burke thereupon threw himself on top of her, and for the space of ten or fifteen minutes kept "one hand under her nose, and the other under her chin." She then appeared to be dead, but Burke, to make sure, kept his hand across her mouth for a little longer.

Hare was careful to explain that he had taken no part in the old woman's death, but had been sitting all the time upon a chair, although as Cockburn was quick to point out, "without stirring one hand to help her." His wife and Helen M'Dougal, he said, had both run into the passage when they heard Mrs Docherty scream as Burke grasped her; they did not come back until everything was over and the body covered with straw. Burke then went out to tell Paterson that he had something to take to Surgeons' Square, and arrangements were made for the delivery that evening of the tea-chest at Dr Knox's—with the result that Burke and M'Dougal were arrested that night, and Hare and his wife on the following morning.

Mrs Hare was then sworn in by Lord Meadowbank in the same manner as Hare. Throughout the trial she carried in her arms an infant in the throes of whooping-cough, whose every paroxysm seemed to "fire her with intenser anger and impatience." Under examination she told practically the same story as her husband about the last hours of Mrs Docherty, adding only that as soon as they saw the old woman with Burke on top of her she and M'Dougal "were both alarmed, and fled out of the house" staying in the passage for about fifteen minutes. When Mrs Hare returned she asked no questions, she "had a supposition" that Mrs Docherty had been murdered, as she had "seen such tricks before." She had not called the neighbours to help because, she said "it was not likely that I should tell a thing to affect my husband."

After some medical evidence and the reading of the "declarations" of the prisoners, Burke and Helen M'Dougal (which had been made soon after their arrest and contained little truth) the Lord Advocate closed the case for the Crown. After reviewing the evidence Sir William Rae explained the difficulties that had, and indeed still, existed in obtaining medical proof of Mrs Docherty's murder, but submitted that after hearing all the facts and opinions, the members of the jury should have no reasonable doubt in their minds as to the cause of death, but, if they had, they should consider the evidence of Hare and his wife who saw the deed committed. He did not present them as "unexceptionable witnesses . . . assuredly they were great criminals." but the Law accepted their testimony, and at some length Sir William explained why he had taken the course he had in accepting Hare as King's Evidence. It was, he said for the jury to decide "the degree of credit" to which the Hares were entitled, but he pointed out, they had to consider also the evidence of the neighbours. Altogether, as he saw it, there was "a mass of direct and circumstantial evidence" to prove the guilt of William Burke.

The Lord Advocate then turned to the case of Helen M'Dougal, who had been charged as accessory to the crime. In his view she was aware of Burke's intention to commit the crime, and helped him by detaining the woman in the house and plying her with drink; she and Mrs Hare did nothing to help the victim, nor to call the neighbours; it might well be that they stationed themselves in the passage to prevent intrusion. Next morning she did what she could to conceal the murder, even trying to bribe the Grays not to go to the police station. In the light of all this, the Lord Advocate concluded by "demanding in the name of the country, a verdict of guilty against both the prisoners at the bar."

It was now 3 a.m. and although there had been an interval for refreshment at 6 p.m. the trial had already lasted for seventeen hours, but there could be no respite, and Sir James Moncrieff rose to address the jury in defence of Burke. He was confronted by an impossible task, but he made his points clearly and underlined weak spots in the Crown case—such as the lack of positive medical evidence on the cause of death. He begged the jury to put to one side "probability" and "supposition" and concentrate on legal evidence, and to remember that the prisoner was charged "simply and singly" with murder.

Sir James was followed at 5 a.m. by Cockburn, for Helen M'Dougal. Henry Cockburn was then in his fiftieth year, and his address to the jury, together with his masterly cross-examination of the Hares, were the highlights of the trial. Although, by the circumstances in which he found himself and by the ruling of Scots Law, Hare had been able to refuse to answer some of his questions, the mere fact that he did refuse to answer such questions as: "Was this the first murder that you have been concerned in?" and "Was there murder committed in your house in the last October?" did much, as Cockburn himself says, "to impeach the credit of the accomplices."

Cockburn was therefore in a very strategic position when he began to plead "that there is not sufficient credible evidence to convict this woman" Helen M'Dougal. Cockburn's manner of approach was quite different from that of Sir James Moncrieff; he took the human angle, and as extenuating circumstances, said that Helen M'Dougal

> "in a moral sense, was as completely under Burke's influence as any wife could be to any husband. Great allowance, therefore must be made in judging of her conduct, from the control which he may have exercised over her; and for the interest which she may naturally, and most properly, have had in concealing her husband's crimes."

His peroration was dramatic:

> "What M'Dougal is endangered by, is, the cry of the public for a victim. . . . Let the public rage as it pleases. It is the duty, and the glory of juries, always to hold the balance the more steadily, the more that the storm of prejudice is up. The time will come when these prejudices will die away. In that hour, you will have to recollect whether you this day yielded to them or not; a question which you cannot answer to the satisfaction of your own minds, unless you can then recall, or at least are certain that you now feel, legal grounds for convicting this woman, after deducting all the evidence of the Hares, and all your extrajudicial impressions. If you have such evidence,—convict her. If you have not,—your safest course is to find that the libel is not proven."

An hour later, at 6 a.m. the Lord Justice-Clerk began his summing-up. As Roughead comments, he reviewed "the whole evidence with a minuteness at once exhaustive, and at that hour presumably exhausting." His final charge to the jury was that:

> "If the jury had doubts,—reasonable and rational doubts on the subject of the prisoners' guilt, or either of them,—they were bound to give them the benefit of these doubts, without allowing their own minds to be influenced or carried away by any prejudice or popular clamour that might exist against them. On the other hand, if the jury were, in their consciences, satisfied of the guilt of the prisoners, they must return a verdict accordingly."

At half-past eight on Christmas morning the jury retired. Fifty minutes later they returned and their foreman gave their verdict:

Burke. Guilty.

Helen M'Dougal. Not proven.

Upon which Burke at once turned to her saying kindly, and possibly with some surprise "Nelly, you are out of the scrape." Helen M'Dougal had indeed been "much agitated, and was drowned in tears" at this point. Burke on the contrary, listened to his own sentence with "unshaken firmness, not a muscle of his features was discomposed." After some legal formalities his sentence was "proposed" by Lord Meadowbank—the usual fate of a murderer—then the Lord Justice-Clerk put on the black cap and read it aloud:

". . . William Burke to be carried from the bar back to the Tolbooth of Edinburgh, therein to be detained, and to be fed upon bread and water only, in terms of an Act of Parliament passed in the 25th year of H.M. King George II . . . until Wednesday, 28th January, and upon that day to be taken forth of the said Tolbooth to the common place of execution, in the Lawnmarket of Edinburgh, and then and there, between the hours of eight and ten o'clock before noon of the said day, to be hanged by the neck by the hands of the common executioner, upon a gibbet, until he be dead, and his body thereafter to be delivered to Dr Alexander Monro, Professor of Anatomy in the University of Edinburgh, to be by him publicly dissected and anatomized, in terms of the said Act; and ordain all his moveable goods and gear to be escheat and inbrought to His Majesty's use, which is pronounced for doom. And may Almighty God have mercy on your soul."

9

Helen M'Dougal, who certainly owed her life to the eloquence of Cockburn, was set free within twenty-four hours, but her Counsel had not over-estimated the popular "prejudice" against her. Very foolishly she returned to her old haunts at the West Port, where she encountered such a hostile crowd that she was glad to seek police protection. Everywhere she went she was recognised and mobbed; at Newcastle the police had again to rescue her, but after that all trace of her is lost, although she is reputed to have died in Australia in 1868.

Mrs Hare was released on 19 January 1829. She was recognised in the Old Town, and might have been lynched had she not been carrying her still whooping infant; as it was, she was pelted with snow-balls and had to be rescued by the police. She then went to Glasgow to try to board a ship for Ireland, but she was recognised on the Broomielaw and stoned. Thereupon the police again took her under their protection and made arrangements for her transport to Ireland; she sailed from Greenock for Belfast on 12 February.

The two women prisoners thus disappeared from the scene, but the public were still out for the blood of Hare—and of Dr Knox, and the newspapers constantly added fuel to the fire:

> The conviction of Burke alone will not satisfy either the law or the country. (*Caledonian Mercury*, 27 Dec. 1828.)
>
> All the anatomical teachers, therefore, and others who use *cadavera* for their classes, both within and without the University, ought to be examined as to the manner in which they are accustomed to receive their subjects. And, in particular, the students and assistants (during the last two sessions) of one gentleman, whose name has unfortunately been too much mixed up with the late proceedings, ought to undergo an examination as to the quarter whence bodies were procured—the state in which they were received—the *manner* in which they were dissected, etc. . . . The present impression on the minds of the people is, that one gentleman stands in the same relation to Burke and Hare that the murderers of Banquo did to Macbeth. This impression, we believe and trust, is ill-founded; but the fact of its existence, which cannot be disputed, should induce him to demand an inquiry; and the other teachers ought also to demand it, in order to vindicate their reputation from the foul suspicions which attach to it in the public mind. (*Caledonian Mercury*, 29 Dec. 1828.)
>
> Ever shall we regret that M'Dougal was not made to pay the penalty of her crime upon the gibbet. We cannot understand upon what principle she was acquitted. . . . Justice demands . . . more victims shall be immolated upon her altar. The public voice also calls for other sacrifices. (*Edinburgh Weekly Chronicle*, 31 Dec. 1828.)

The public voice certainly was calling, and calling loudly, for other sacrifices, but the Lord Advocate was in a very awkward position. Hare had turned King's Evidence on receiving an official promise that he would not be tried for his part in the three murders in the indictment, and that being so, the Lord Advocate decided that he was "legally barred" from prosecuting him for the murder of either Mary Paterson or Daft Jamie. He added "that he should strongly feel such a proceeding, upon his part as dishonourable in itself, unworthy of his office, and highly injurious to the administration of justice."

When news of his decision became known, public indignation knew no bounds. A fund was raised, Francis Jeffrey was engaged as Counsel, and private criminal proceedings were put in motion against Hare by Mrs and Miss Wilson, the mother and sister of Daft Jamie. Hare, thereupon, petitioned first the Sheriff and then the High Court, that this warrant should be recalled and himself set at liberty; in view of the assurances he had received, these proceedings against him were "incompetent, irregular, oppressive and illegal." The High Court remitted the matter to the Lord Advocate on 26 January. This, then, was Hare's position on the eve of Burke's execution, the date of which had been fixed for 28 January.

The day dawned wet and stormy, torrents of rain in fact were falling, but from a very early hour a crowd of over 20,000 spectators was gathering in the Lawnmarket; a crowd of cheerful, happy people, who looked as though they were waiting for "some splendid procession or agreeable exhibition." The scaffold had been erected in the High Street, at the north-west corner of the County Buildings, and when at 2 a.m. the workmen put the finishing touches to it, three such tremendous cheers went up from the waiting crowd, that they could be heard in Princes Street.

Seats in all the windows of the old houses with a view of the scaffold had been sold to "fashionable" Edinburgh at prices varying from five to twenty-five shillings. Charles Kirkpatrick Sharpe had booked seats for Sir Walter Scott and himself but Scott may not have gone with him. The fact is not recorded in the *Journal*; all that Scott wrote there was:

> Burke the murderer hanged this morning. The mob, which was immense, demanded Knox and Hare, but, though greedy for more victims, received with shouts the solitary wretch who found his way to the gallows out of five or six who seem not less guilty than he.

Punctually at 8 a.m. Burke had appeared, walking towards the scaffold with firm step, leaning on the arm of Mr Reid, a Roman Catholic priest, but the "loud and simultaneous shout" with which the crowd greeted him seemed to disturb him. The clamour, indeed, even when he knelt in prayer with the priest, must have been stupendous as "yells of execration burst from the spectators." There were shouts also for Hare and Knox: "Hare! Hare! bring out Hare!" "Hang Knox!" "He's a *noxious* morsel!" Then, as Burke made ready, and the executioner adjusted the rope, there were further shouts of "Burke him," "Give him no rope!" "Do the same for Hare!"

It was not an edifying scene. At 8.15 Burke gave the signal, and "amidst the most tremendous shouts died almost without a struggle." Even worse were the scenes when, after about an hour, his body was cut down, and only a large force of police and strong barriers held the crowd back; while a scramble took place among the assistants under the scaffold for portions of the rope, which was sold at 2s. 6d. an inch.

> 'Midst a fiendish yell, Burke danced to hell;
> 'Gainst him the door old Satan locks.
> Says he, This place you shan't disgrace;
> Go back to earth and dwell with Knox!

The next day the body was taken to the University for the carrying out of the second part of the sentence (which in this case so aptly fitted the crime): dissection by Professor Monro—a legal act, as Burke had been a murderer. In the University Quadrangle there were further scenes. The lecture and dissection (of the brain) had been due to begin at one o'clock, but so many of the public had come early, before the doors were opened, that the lecture-room was soon filled to capacity. Two thousand students then arrived, and were furious when they found there were no places for them, and they became even more furious when they discovered that the police had been called to keep them in order. Soon the students had the police hemmed into a corner, and there was a general mêlée. It was lucky that Professor Christison happened to pass by at that moment; acting on his own initiative, he promised the students that they should file past the corpse later that afternoon in parties of fifty, on his personal guarantee for their good conduct. During the next two days the privilege was extended to 40,000 of the populace, who, like the students, "behaved with the utmost decorum." Burke's body was afterwards dissected, and the skeleton now hangs in the Anatomical Museum of Edinburgh University.

Sir Walter Scott's entry in his *Journal* for 31 January 1829 is good comment:

> The corpse of the Murderer Burke is now lying in state at the College, in the anatomical class, and all the world flock to see him. Who is he that says that we are not ill to please in our objects of curiosity. The strange means by which the wretch made money are scarce more disgusting than the eager curiosity with which the public have licked up all the carrion details of this business.

Before his death Burke had made two confessions, which were published about ten days later. One was a journalistic "scoop" by the newspaper *Edinburgh Evening Courant*; it was genuine, but nobody knew how it had been obtained. The other was "official"; it had been made on 3 January in the presence of the Sheriff, the Procurator-Fiscal, and the Sheriff-Clerk, to which was added a postscript, or "supplement," on 22 January. Both confessions contained accounts of the sixteen murders, which Burke declared to be all that the partnership had been connected with, but he attributed to Hare a good share of the blame which Hare had laid on him in his evidence, although he did state that neither Mrs Hare nor Helen M'Dougal had been in any way concerned with the murders. He also made it clear, which was an important point for the Lord Advocate, that he and Hare were working on their own and had no other associates, and he made a definite statement:

> that suffocation was not suggested to them by any person as a mode of killing, but occurred to Hare on the first occasion before mentioned, and was continued afterwards because it was effectual, and showed no marks.

This was helpful to Dr Knox as there had been some very unpleasant innuendoes in the New Year's Day edition of the *Caledonian Mercury* that Burke had been "tutored" by some scientific person as to the mode of committing the crime.

The *Courant* confession, however, was the more important to Dr Knox as its last paragraph specifically stated that:

> Burke declares that Dr Knox never encouraged him, neither taught him or encouraged him to murder any person, neither any of his assistants, that worthy gentleman, Mr Fergusson, was the only man that ever mentioned anything about the bodies. He enquired where we got the young woman Paterson.

These confessions were published on 7 February, and by then the Lord Advocate had made up his mind what he was going to do with Hare. Two days before, on 5 February, he had released him. Not without due deliberation had the Lord Advocate let his prisoner go. On 2 February he had appeared to represent the Crown, together with the Solicitor-General and three Advocates-Depute, before five High Court judges (Lords Gillies, Pitmilly, Meadowbank, Mackenzie, and Alloway) presided over by the Lord Justice-Clerk, who argued at length the legal pros and cons as to whether Hare could or could not be tried for the murder of Daft Jamie. Duncan M'Neil and Hugh Bruce appeared for Hare, and Francis Jeffrey, Miller, and Sandford for the Wilsons. The decision (four to two—Lords Gillies and Alloway dissenting) was that Hare could not be prosecuted for the murder of James Wilson, that the proceedings against him should be quashed, and he himself set at liberty. Although the Wilsons made another bid to bring Hare to trial by means of a civil action, they finally abandoned it, and Hare was set free.

When he was released on Thursday, 5 February, the authorities remembered the rough justice administered by the crowds to his wife and to Helen M'Dougal, and did what they could to get him over the Border as quickly as possible. At 8 p.m. on that Thursday night the head turnkey of the Calton Jail took him, muffled in an old cloak and with his hat pulled over his eyes, in a hackney coach to Newington, which was a stopping-place for the south-bound mail-coach. When it arrived the turnkey saw him aboard, and to avert suspicion, called out loudly "Good-bye, Mr Black; I wish you well home." The first stop was at Noble-house on the Edinburgh-Dumfries road, where the passengers got out for supper at the inn, and there, after supper in the inn parlour, Hare by mischance was recognised by a fellow-passenger.

There are two versions of the story of what happened next. One states that the gentleman who had been sitting next Hare inside the coach on the first stage from Edinburgh, was so horrified to discover at the inn who his companion was that he himself preferred to finish the journey as an outside passenger, notwithstanding the fact that it was a bitterly cold night.

But the *Dumfries Courier* of 10 February 1829 reported that Hare was recognised at the inn by no less a person than Mr Douglas Sandford, who had been junior counsel for the Wilsons and who, by a strange coincidence, was travelling on that very coach. He insisted that Hare should no longer enjoy the amenities of an "inside" passenger, ordered him to take a seat outside, and revealed his identity to his fellow-travellers, with the result that when the mail stopped at the King's Arms in the High Street of Dumfries, the inn was soon surrounded by a crowd of 8,000 persons who quickly became hostile. Hare's life was probably saved only by the speedy intervention of the police and the quick thinking of the city fathers. They despatched the mail coach to Portpatrick (which was supposed to be Hare's destination) on time, but empty—having already sent the passengers on ahead in a gig. By distracting the attention of the people, and getting Hare out by a back window and into a chaise, they deposited him safely in Dumfries prison, which was then beseiged by a noisy crowd who battered the doors and broke the windows. Hastily 100 special constables were enrolled, and at their appearance with batons the unsuccessful, and by now exhausted, crowds melted away. By midnight everything was quiet, and soon afterwards, escorted by a Sheriff's officer and guarded by militiamen, Hare was taken out of the town and set upon the Annan road to find his own way south. By daybreak he was over the Border; on Sunday he was seen two miles south of Carlisle, and that is the last we hear of him, although many years later London nursemaids would point out to "awe-struck" children a certain blind beggar on Oxford Street and tell them that he was William Hare, the murderer.

That, however, was far in the future. What the crowds in Edinburgh knew by the middle of Feburary 1829, was that they had been baulked of their prey. Mrs Hare was on her way to

PLATE 5

Caricature of Dr Knox, drawn at the time of the murders.

From *Noxiana*, by courtesy of the Trustees of the National Library of Scotland.

Ireland, and now Hare and Helen M'Dougal were lost without trace in industrial England. But in Edinburgh there was still Dr Knox.

On Thursday night, 12 February, large crowds assembled on the Calton Hill and set out for the doctor's house in Newington, carrying with them a life-size effigy of the doctor, clad recognisably in a gaudy waistcoat, etc., and bearing a label, "Knox, the associate of the infamous Hare." When they reached Newington they hanged the effigy by its neck to the branch of a tree, and then tried to make a bonfire of it; this failing, "amidst loud huzzas" they tore the figure to pieces. There is no doubt that they would have done as much to Knox if they had caught him. As it was, they trampled on the flower-beds of his garden and destroyed his railings, "shouting wrathfully, and blending his name with those of the West Port murderers." When the police appeared on the scene they were stoned, several of them being injured and most of the windows of Dr Knox's house were broken.

Dr Knox behaved as might have been expected of one who had seen service in South Africa and was a crack shot. Seeing that the mob was out for his blood, he calmly walked out by the back of his house, and passed through the seething streets to seek shelter at the home of a friend, having taken the precaution of wearing a military cloak and arming himself with sword, pistols and Highland dirk. To his astonished friend, Dr Adams, he said on his arrival: "You see my arms, and had I been called upon to defend myself, I would have measured a score of the brutes."[42]

There were riots elsewhere in Edinburgh that night, in the High Street and Cowgate, when the police made about twenty arrests. It was also rumoured that there might be another demonstration at Portobello, and this actually took place—Dr Knox's effigy being burned on the site of the old gibbet. The comment of the *Edinburgh Weekly Chronicle* is worth quoting at length, as it shows to what an extent Dr Knox had the bad will of the press:

Since the grand spectacle of the execution of Dr Knox in effigy was exhibited, about twenty-three of those concerned in it have been fined

---

[42] Lonsdale, *op. cit.*, p. 110.

in sums of from five to forty shillings . . . all defrayed out of a stock purse previously collected.

Another auto-da-fe is meditated; on which occasion the cavalcade will move in the direction of Portobello, where, it is supposed, the Doctor burrows at night. As we have said before, the agitation of public feeling will never subside till the city be released of this man's presence, or until his innocence be manifested. In justice to himself, if he is innocent, in justice to the public, if he is guilty, he ought to be put upon trial.

Knox refused to be intimidated by this mass violence, and although the entrance to Surgeons' Square was picketed he never missed a single lecture, and thereby won the affection and admiration of all his students, who welcomed him with cheers. On one occasion they became alarmed when the yells of the howling crowd outside became audible in the class-room, and Dr Knox, perceiving this, paused and said:

"Gentlemen, you are disquieted by these noises, to which, no doubt, you attach a proper meaning. Do not be alarmed! It is my life, not your's they seek. The assailants of our peace may be big in menace, but they are too cowardly in act to confront such a phalanxed body of gentlemen as I see before me. How little I regard these ruffians you may well judge, for, in spite of daily warnings and the destruction of my property, I have met you at every hour of lecture during the session; and I am not aware that my efforts to convey instruction have been less clear or less acceptable to you."[43]

He then added a topical note to his lecture by talking of Vesalius, the founder of modern Anatomy (who suffered death at the hands of the Spanish Inquisition) "and others who had suffered martyrdom in their zeal in the cause of Anatomy." Dr Knox at that moment might have almost welcomed martyrdom. He probably expected to be stoned, like some of those others, but what fate had in store for him was martyrdom even more protracted. As Lonsdale truly says:

The guilty culprit Burke met his fate at the gallows of the Lawnmarket; but the brunt of a lasting and national reproach fell upon the head of the innocent Robert Knox.

---

[43] Lonsdale, *op. cit.*, p. 111.

10

Dr Knox had not been called as a witness at Burke's trial, and during it and for two months thereafter he maintained a dignified silence. He was determined to say nothing that could be "hurtful to science" and indeed, if he were to speak, he could say nothing that the hounds of Edinburgh, who were baying for his blood, were likely to understand.

He had undertaken an occupational risk common to all the teachers of anatomy in Britain who wished to provide a good education for their pupils; the others had been lucky, he had been unlucky—that was the only difference.

Nor would anything that Knox could say have advanced the cause he had so much at heart, the passing of an Act of Parliament to legalise the supply of "subjects." The Government already had in its possession the Report of the Select Committee on Anatomy, and what could Knox add to the evidence printed in its pages only six months earlier?

Because of the distance from London, neither he nor any of the Edinburgh surgeons had been called before that Committee, but all the points they might have wished to raise had been included in the testimony of Sir Astley Cooper and his colleagues.

Under examination Sir Astley had given, in no uncertain terms, his views on the value of anatomical studies:

> I should reply that without dissection there can be no anatomy, and that anatomy is our polar star, for, without anatomy a surgeon can do nothing, certainly nothing well. . . . I would not remain in a room with a man who attempted to perform an operation in surgery who was unacquainted with anatomy, unless he would be directed by others; he must mangle the living, if he has not operated on the dead. . . . The cause which you gentlemen are now supporting, is not our cause, but your's; you must employ medical men, whether they be ignorant or informed; but if you have none but ignorant medical men, it is you who suffer from it; and the fact is, that the want of subjects will very soon lead to your becoming the unhappy victims of operations founded and performed in ignorance.

In answer to a question:

> "Is it not distressing to men of character, as the teachers in the schools of Anatomy are, to be obliged to have recourse to a violation of the law

in order to obtain a supply of bodies and perform their duty towards their pupils?"

Sir Astley replied:

"The great difficulty teachers have to contend with, is the management of these persons, and it is distressing to our feelings that we are obliged to employ very very faulty agents to obtain a desirable end."

In the light of what was to come, the evidence of Mr Brodie, surgeon at St. George's, is of considerable interest:

"Are you aware of the character of the men who supply the bodies by exhumation?"

"Yes, they are as bad as any in society, and when I consider their characters I think it is a dangerous thing to society that they should be able to get ten guineas for a body."

Sir Henry Halford, President of the Royal College of Physicians, went further, and said:

"When there is a difficulty in obtaining bodies, and their value is so great, you absolutely throw a temptation in the way of these men to commit murder for the purpose of selling the bodies of their victims."

There was no doubt of it, the anatomists had all been living on the edge of the same volcano. So there was a certain irony in the fact that the full blaze of publicity, when it came, should have shone not on the outspoken little Blue Book of 1828, but on Robert Knox, the silent Scot; the man, who, only a few months previously, had counselled, in the interests of science, "the making of these matters as little public as possible."

It is easy to understand that Knox's friends disliked, and possibly misunderstood, his policy of silence; they wished for something more positive, some rousing vindication of his innocence. Without telling him, they asked a Mr Ellis to make an enquiry into all the known facts and then took Counsel's opinion on this report, with the result that a private committee (sanctioned by Knox) "of persons of undoubted weight and character" was set up to investigate the truth or falsehood of the rumours in circulation regarding him.

It all seems rather amateurish and unnecessary, and it might have been just as well if Knox's friends had not tried to save him from himself, but on the other hand there was more than a whispering campaign going on against him in the early months of 1829. In the House of Commons, for instance, on 8 May, Mr W. Smith

complained of a letter signed "Palestinus," in which it was said that Dr Knox, of Edinburgh, was guilty of the grossest and most intolerable criminality, and that he was unworthy to be trusted. If Dr Knox, of whom he knew nothing, did not deserve this, it was to be reprobated in the highest degree. The character of a man whose reputation depended upon his character ought not to be violated.

In fact Robert Knox must have had almost superhuman self-control to have kept silence as he did in the midst of so much provocation.

One of the most influential people in the ranks against Dr Knox was Sir Walter Scott; the entry in his *Journal* for 14 January 1829 reads:

I called on Mr Robison and instructed him to call a meeting of the Council of the Royal Society, as Mr Knox proposes to read an essay on some dissections. A bold proposal truly from one who has had so lately the boldness of trading so deep in human flesh. I will oppose his reading in the present circumstances if I should stand alone, but I hope he will be wrought upon to withdraw his essay or postpone it at least. It is very bad taste to push himself forward just now.

Poor Knox, who must in his present position have given little heed to the criteria of good or bad taste, refused to withdraw his paper, but "suffered the reading to be postponed." He surely must have made some appeal to Scott's legal experience, as the next *Journal* entry is much less severe; it almost sounds as though Knox had lent him the Report of the Select Committee:

15th January 1829. There is some great error in the law of the subject. If it was left to itself many bodies would be imported from France and Ireland, and doubtless many would be found in our hospitals for the service of anatomical science.

All the same it was unlikely that Scott would consent to serve on that unofficial committee to assess Dr Knox's innocence. On 23 January he was approached by Mr George Sinclair of Ulbster (son of Sir John Sinclair):

His business with me was to invite me to be one of a committee who were to sit as Mr Knox's friends in a Committee of enquiry on his late traffic with the West Port. In other words to lend a hand to whitewash this much to be suspected individual. But he shall ride off on no back of mine. I feel no call to mix myself in the business at all . . . I will travel in no such boat.

The committee, nevertheless, was constituted without Sir Walter, and was by no means a gathering of "Mr Knox's friends." It consisted of Mr George Sinclair, Mr M. P. Brown (Advocate), Mr James Russell (Professor of Clinical Surgery), Mr J. Shaw Stewart (Advocate), Dr W. P. Alison (Professor of the Theory of Physic), Sir George Ballingall (Professor of Military Surgery), Sir W. Hamilton, Bart. (Professor of Universal History), Mr Thomas Allan (banker in Edinburgh), and in the Chair, Mr John Robison (Secretary to the Royal Society of Edinburgh).

This committee worked diligently for six weeks and produced a unanimous report. They had, they said, been

> . . . readily furnished with all which they required from Dr Knox himself; and though they had failed in some attempts to procure evidence they had in most quarters succeeded in obtaining it, and especially from those persons who had been represented to them as having spoken the most confidently in support of these rumours.

The report was a long one, and went very thoroughly into the various charges that had been made against Knox. The first paragraph stated emphatically that the committee "firmly believed" that neither Dr Knox nor his assistants knew that murder had been committed in obtaining the "subjects." They were also of the opinion, "after most anxious enquiry," that no suspicion of murder ever existed in Dr Knox's mind, even though the bodies were brought to him so soon after death, and with no external marks of disease, indeed the lack of such marks increased the difficulty of ascertaining the cause of death. The committee also had evidence that no suggestions of murder had been made by any of Knox's assistants, nor by any member of his very large class, while the "complete publicity" with which Knox's establishment was managed, and his anxiety to lay the "subjects" before his students as quickly as possible indicated that "he had no suspicion of the atrocious means by which they had been procured." Further, the committee stated that it had been proved to their satisfaction that the "subjects" brought by Burke and Hare were dissected in the same "protracted manner" as the others, and that no attempt had been made to mutilate or disfigure them with a view to concealing their identity.

The committee then commented on the belief which Knox was known to hold, that bodies might be procured by purchase, without crime, "from the relatives or connections of deceased persons of the lowest ranks of society," and gave the view that "Dr Knox acted on this opinion in a very incautious manner," as it led him "to give a ready ear to the plausible stories of Burke . . . who always represented himself as engaged in negotiations of that description, and occasionally asked and obtained money in advance to enable him and his associate to conclude bargains."

Although recognising that at this time Dr Knox was a very busy man, the committee regretted that he had seen fit to depute the reception of "subjects" to his students and porter, who made no particular enquiries of the persons bringing the bodies "on the understanding (common to Dr Knox, with some other anatomists) that it would only tend to diminish or divert the supply of subjects." Here the committee thought that greater vigilance might have been employed, especially as the bodies had never been interred.

The conclusion the Committee reached was that:

> The extent to which Dr Knox can be blamed, on account of transactions with Burke and Hare, is, that by this laxity of the regulations under which bodies were received into his rooms, he unintentionally gave a degree of facility to the disposal of the victims of their crimes, which, under better regulations, would not have existed, and which is doubtless matter of deep and lasting regret, not only to himself, but to all who have reflected on the importance, and are therefore interested in the prosecution of the study of anatomy. But while they point out this circumstance as the only ground of censure which they can discover in the conduct of Dr Knox, it is fair to observe that perhaps the recent disclosures have made it appear reprehensible to many who would not otherwise have adverted to its possible consequences.

In short, it is easy to be wise after the event. This report was handed to Knox on 16 March 1829. He, and indeed the committee, had always intended that the proceedings should be private, but as they had come to the ears of the press, Dr Knox, on 17 March, sent a letter to the editor of the *Caledonian Mercury*:

Sir,

I regret troubling either you or the public with anything personal, but I cannot be insensible of the feelings of my friends, or of the character of the profession to which I have the honour of belonging. Had I alone been concerned, I should never have thought of obtruding on the public by this communication.

I have a class of above 400 pupils. No person can be at the head of such an establishment without necessarily running the risk of being imposed upon by those who furnish the material of their science to anatomical teachers; and, accordingly, there is hardly any such person who has not occasionally incurred odium or suspicion from his supposed accession to those violations of the law, without which anatomy can scarcely now be practised. That I should have become an object of popular prejudice, therefore, since mine happened to be the establishment with which Burke and Hare chiefly dealt, was nothing more than what I had to expect. But if means had not been purposely taken, and most keenly persevered in, to misrepresent facts and to inflame the public mind, that prejudice would at least have stood on right ground, and would ultimately have passed away, by its being seen that I had been exposed to a mere misfortune which would almost certainly have occurred to anybody else who had been in my situation.

But every effort has been employed to convert my misfortune into positive and intended personal guilt of the most dreadful character. Scarcely any individual has ever been the object of more systematic or atrocious attacks than I have been. Nobody acquainted with this place requires to be told from what quarter these have proceeded.

I allowed them to go on for months without taking the slightest notice of them; and I was inclined to adhere to this system, especially as the public authorities by never charging me with any offence, gave the whole attestation they could that they had nothing to charge me with. But my friends interfered for me. Without consulting me, they directed an agent to institute the most rigid and unsparing examination into the facts. I was totally unacquainted with this gentleman, but I understood that in naming Mr Ellis they named a person whose character is a sufficient pledge for the propriety of his proceedings.

The result of his inquiries was laid before the Dean of Faculty and another Counsel, who were asked what ought to be done. These gentlemen gave it as their opinion that the evidence was completely satisfactory, and that there was no want of actionable matter, but that there was one ground on which it was my duty to resist the temptation of going into a Court of law. This was, that the disclosures of the most innocent proceedings even of the best-conducted dissecting-room must always shock the public and be hurtful to science. But they recommended that a few persons of undoubted weight and character should be asked to investigate the matter, in order that, if I deserved it, an attestation might be given to me which would be more satisfactory to my friends than any mere statements of mine could be expected to be. This led to the formation of a Committee, which was never meant by me to be anything but private. But the fact of its sitting soon got into the newspapers, and hence the necessity under which I am placed of explaining how that proceeding, in which the public has been made to take an interest, has terminated.

I have been on habits of friendship with some of the Committee, with others of them I have been acquainted, and some of them I don't even know by sight. I took no charge whatever of their proceedings. In order that there might be no pretence for saying the truth was obstructed from fear, I gave a written protection to every person to say what he chose about or against me. The extent to which this was in some instances taken advantage of will probably not be soon forgotten by those who witnessed it.

After a severe and laborious investigation of about six weeks, the result is contained in the following report, which was put into my hands last night. It is signed by every member of the Committee except one, who ceased to act long before the evidence was completed.

I cannot be supposed to be a candid judge of my own case, and therefore it is extremely probable that any opinion of mine on the last view adopted by the Committee is incorrect and theirs right. If it be so, I most willingly submit to the censure they have inflicted, and shall hold it my duty to profit from it by due care hereafter. My consolation is, that I have at least not been obstinate in my errors, and that no sanction has ever been given in any fair quarter to the more serious imputations by which it has been the interest of certain persons to assail me. Candid men will judge of me according to the situation in which I was placed at the time, and not according to the wisdom which has unexpectedly been acquired since.

This is the very first time that I have ever made any statement to the public in my own vindication, and it shall be the last. It would be unjust to the authors of the former calumnies to suppose that they would not renew them now. I can only assure them that, in so far as I am concerned, they will renew them in vain.

I have the honour to be, etc.,

R. Knox.

It was his first and last vindication; he made no attempt to answer the attack made upon him in the March edition of *Blackwood's Magazine* by "Christopher North" (the pseudonym of John Wilson, Professor of Moral Philosophy in the University of Edinburgh) although it must have strengthened his belief that there was a University clique working against him.

This article by the erudite Professor, which so exactly represented the popular Edinburgh opinion of the time, makes, in retrospect, rather strange reading. In the first place it seems to reflect an almost sadistic gloating over the execution of Burke. The writer, for instance, says frankly that he was glad to hear that the hangman fastened the knot "behind his neck to keep him in pain." He also calls the *Courant* correspondent a "driveller" and an "idiot" because he had ventured to comment adversely on the conduct of the mob at the hanging. On the contrary, writes Christopher North, the people on that occasion "in spite of clerical and lay authorities, behaved in every way worthy of their national character." The thought of Dr Knox, and "Dr Knox's shambles" produced the Professor's finest flights of rhetoric:

> Dr Knox stands arraigned at the bar of the public, his accuser being—human nature.
>
> He is ordered to open his mouth and speak, or be for ever dumb. Sixteen uninterred bodies—for the present I sink the word murdered—have been purchased, within nine months, by him and his, from the two brutal wretches who lived by that trade. Let him prove, to the conviction of all reasonable men, that it was impossible he could suspect any evil,—that the practice of selling the dead was so general as to be almost universal among the poor of this city—and that he knew it to be so—and then we shall send his vindication abroad on all the winds of heaven. . . .
>
> If wholly and entirely innocent, he need not fear that he shall be able to establish his innocence. Give me the materials, and I will do so for him;—but he is not now the victim of some wild and foolish calumny; the whole world shudders at the transactions; and none but a base, blind, brutal beast can at this moment dare to declare, "Dr Knox stands free from all suspicion of being accessory to murder."

Not content with this, Professor Wilson went on to attack Dr Knox's students:

> The shouts and cheers at Burke's appearance on the scaffold were right—human nature being constituted as it is; but the shouts and cheers on Dr Knox's appearance at the table where so many of Burke's victims had been dissected, after having been murdered, were "horrible, most horrible," and calculated—whatever may be their effect on more thinking minds—to confirm in those of the populace the conviction that they are all a gang

of murderers together, and determined to insult, in horrid exultation, all the deepest feelings of humanity.

Knox certainly had the consolation of knowing that he had the absolute loyalty of all his students. They "wished to give him a lasting proof of their attachment, by presenting him with a handsome testimonial" but when he heard of this idea Knox tried to dissuade them:

Gentlemen,

When your intention to present me with a piece of plate first reached me I hesitated about interfering, though I did not like it, partly because professions of unwillingness to receive such honours are very apt to be misunderstood, and partly because I was exceedingly fond of the good opinion of my pupils.

But every subsequent reflection has tended to confirm my original feeling, which was that your gratifying design ought not to be carried into effect, and I now feel it my duty to state to you plainly, that I hope you will not persist in it.

You cannot but do me the justice to believe, that I appreciate the affection of my students as I ought. Their kindness has contributed powerfully to uphold me in a situation which has required no ordinary support, and no day can ever arrive in which I shall not recollect their attachment with pride and gratitude. But presents from pupils to masters are in general to be discouraged, and the events which have suggested this occasion to you as an exception are the very circumstances which make me sincerely anxious to decline this expression of your favour.

The absurd imputations against me by which the public has been industriously misled, are viewed by you and all reasonable men as they deserve. But, however extravagant these misrepresentations may be, I have never disguised from myself, nor shall I attempt to disguise from you, that the connection of my establishment with the late atrocities, however accidental, is a very severe misfortune; insomuch that, though utterly unconscious at the time of anything wrong having been done, yet the very recollection of these shocking occurrences must be ever painful to me.

In this situation I am unwilling to receive any token of your friendship which must be associated in my own mind, with the heaviest calamity of my life, and which, moreover, I am perfectly aware, cannot at present be accompanied by the sympathy of the public.

Allow me therefore to say I shall consider your abandoning your design as a stronger proof of your attachment than your ever having formed it.

With the warmest wishes for your happiness, believe me very gratefully,

Yours, etc.,

R. KNOX.[44]

---

[44] *Scotsman*, 25 Mar. 1829.

The students, nonetheless, "could not forego the gratification of carrying their design into effect." On 11 April 1829, they presented Knox with a handsome gold vase, and a letter in which they said:

> We have deeply sympathised with you during the mental sufferings which you must have experienced in consequence of circumstances on which we are unwilling to dwell. That you should now stand acquitted of every imputation affecting your character, must gratify, but cannot surprise us. The public voice has at length exonerated you from charges of which we who know you from the first moment felt the injustice.

But the *Scotsman*, in reporting the gift, coldly described it as "injudicious," and this chilly attitude was on the whole representative of Edinburgh opinion. "Robert Knox," said Sir Robert Christison, "never recovered in Edinburgh society from the stigma which thus attached to him." "Robert Knox," also said Sir Robert Christison, "was notoriously deficient in principle and in heart . . . exactly the person to blind himself against suspicion and fall into blamable carelessness." But he did have the grace to add: "it was absurd to charge him with anything worse."

Although Edinburgh persisted in seeing Dr Knox as "a one-eyed obliquity" and as a man "deficient in principle and in heart," there is no reason to think that this is necessarily correct. There is no reason to doubt Knox's sincerity when he told his students that the "very recollection" of what had happened would be "ever painful" to him. Nor were his students likely to be wrong when they spoke of the mental sufferings which he must have endured. Before the public eye, however, Knox's iron self-control was never shaken. In fact in all these months there is only one record of it having failed him, and that was when he was walking one day with his friend, Dr Adams, in one of the Edinburgh parks:

> They talked to a little girl who was playing there and at length Dr Knox gave her a penny and said, "Now, my dear, you and I will be friends. Would you come and live with me if you got a whole penny every day?" "No," said the child, "you would, may be, sell me to Dr Knox." The anatomist started back with a painfully stunned expression, his features began to twitch convulsively and tears appeared in his eyes.

Reference has been made by writers to the "tragic personality" of Robert Knox. Dr James A. Ross and Dr Hugh W. Y. Taylor in an interesting paper contributed in 1955 to the *Journal of the History of Medicine and Allied Sciences* go further and expand that sense of tragedy. They see proof in the pages of his Ms. Catalogue in the Anatomy Department of Edinburgh University, that Knox, far from being unmoved, was so utterly shattered by the revelation of the Burke and Hare murders that from that moment he ceased all research on human anatomy. This book, 13 × 8 inches, with 132 pages, appears to be the catalogue of Knox's own museum of Comparative Anatomy and Human Pathology, and it covers roughly the period 1827-36. It was written up by three hands, one unknown, one that of Frederick Knox, Robert's "Brother Fred" who assisted with his museum, and the third that of Robert Knox himself. Brother Fred's contribution is mainly a tidy list of specimens with illustrative and sometimes entertaining notes, *e.g.*,

No. 547. Mr Brunel's new plan of tunnelling is founded on the observations of the operations of the Teredo (the *calamitas navioum* of Linnaeus). The tunnel under the River Thames would have been totally impracticable without adapting the system of the shield and indeed the whole *modus operandi* of the Teredo, a small testaceous insect.

No. 568. Skeleton of the Creyfish. Mr Watt invented his flexible water-main or pipe from observing the construction of the tail of the lobster.

Dr Knox's entries are quite different from these. They occur at the other end of the book, are initialled "R.K." and appear to be jottings, but very accurate and careful ones, on any interesting abnormalities or variations which he observed in the dissecting-room; many are illustrated by pen-and-ink sketches, which prove him to have been no mean draughtsman. One of these is of a compound dislocation of the knee after an amputation, another of a "loose body in the elbow joint of a stout young subject," another is a life-size sketch of a diseased larynx and trachea, and so on. All of these notes, say Doctors Ross and Taylor "are models of vivid description and reveal the hand of a master."

But what, in this catalogue, sends a shudder down the spine

of the general reader is that page four contains the heading "Anatomical and Pathological appearances met with in the Dissecting Room during the Winter Session of 1827-28" *i.e.,* many of these case reports must refer to bodies brought by Burke and Hare, although there is no means of identifying them. The notes on them go on for about seventeen pages and then stop abruptly after 1828, and never again do we find Dr Knox making such clear and beautiful memoranda of his discoveries; all that Lonsdale found after his death were "heaps of manuscript written on small pieces of paper, sometimes two subjects on the same sheet of paper, the writing on one side being arranged vertically, and on the other side longitudinally." As Bridie points out in the preface to his play, *The Anatomist*—"stoning the prophets is not so good for their morale as many adepts of martyrdom would have us believe." At any rate the authors of the article on the catalogue give it as their opinion that "the abrupt breaking off of the entries on human anatomy so promisingly begun, bears silent testimony to the tragic interruption of a brilliant career."

When Dr Knox laid aside investigation of human anatomy he must have known, and he was only thirty-six, that he was abandoning his life's work. He had said that the quality of genius lay in discovering "new and unobserved phenomena and detecting new relations in phenomena already observed";[45] he had a spark of that genius and it was to be extinguished. What he might have done, what he might have discovered, if he had been allowed to follow his charted course we can only guess. "It is the original work, the original thought" he said, "which alone is entitled to immortality."[46] Once that immortality might have been his; now, living with his horrible memories and in a censorious world—an atmosphere hostile to original research—it would for ever elude him. The shock he had sustained and the lack of any promise for the future could have broken any man. It is a measure of Robert Knox's stature that he remained undaunted.

[45] *Great Artists and Great Anatomists*, p. 22.
[46] *Op. cit.*, p. 40.

In order to face the world Dr Knox could not afford to weaken. Just as it would have made him appear to be in the wrong had he agreed to Scott's suggestion to withdraw his Royal Society paper, so now he could not alter his usual routine. He continued to work at the Royal College of Surgeons' Museum; even in the first quarter of the year 1829, immediately after Burke's trial, he was diligently arranging the different collections of calculi—which want of room had prevented him from exhibiting to advantage, and, "with great propriety,"[47] so the Curators said on 15 May 1829, he "laid a part of these aside until more ample space in the New Apartments of the College shall enable him to display them."

That was the last commendation Dr Knox was to get from the Curators of the Museum. Thenceforth he received not praise but constant nagging criticism which showed how anxious the Surgeons were to be rid of their now too notorious Conservator. It cannot be by pure chance that the first attacks on him appear to coincide with the election on 12 September 1829 of his old enemy, James Syme, as a Curator of the Museum.[48] His hand was shown pretty clearly at the meeting in August of the following year, when the Curators suddenly took their duty towards the College to heart in a most active manner. In spite of Dr Knox having reported "both collections in a good state of preservation" and that the Museums "had suffered no damage during the year" the Curators stated that:

> Conceiving that they owed it to the College to institute an annual examination themselves into the state of the collections under their charge have this week commenced a minute inspection of the preparations, the result of which will be announced in their next report.

A work of supererogation which could only be interpreted as a veiled insult to Dr Knox.

[47] Unless otherwise stated, the quotations in this chapter are taken from R.C.S. (Ed) Minute Books 1829-31.

[48] Syme was now running his own surgical hospital at Minto House. His temper had not improved since 1824 and he had been refused a surgeonship at the Royal Infirmary " lest he and Liston should quarrel openly in the institution." In 1833 he became Professor of Clinical Surgery at Edinburgh University.

That Dr Knox was being deliberately slighted and cold-shouldered by his College colleagues after the Burke and Hare scandal is made clear in a letter which he addressed to the Royal College of Surgeons of Edinburgh and which is now in the Museum of that College. It reveals that even essential information concerning his classes was not being transmitted to him:

> 10 Surgeons' Square,
> 30 November 1829.
>
> Dear Sir,
>
> I am requested to apply to you for the exact copy of a regulation passed by the Royal College in August last, with regard to the registration of those students who had no funds to fee their classes before the close of the Album, Dr Gairdner informs me that the College passed some law, but which they determined should not be printed. Now altho' it would have been preferable that I had been aware of this law when the Registration commenced instead of when it has terminated, yet it would be as well that I am acquainted with it.
>
> I am, Dear Sir,
> Your most obedient servant,
> R. KNOX.

By the early months of 1831 there was open war between James Syme and Dr Knox. This is described in detail in the *History of the Royal College of Surgeons of Edinburgh* by Creswell, who must have had access to now unobtainable documents.

Syme considered that he had been treated without due respect by Dr Knox—apparently over some minor matter of putting up a preparation in the manner desired by its donor, a fact which Syme considered should have been explained to him. A less irascible man than he might have hesitated to quarrel fiercely over such a small point, but Syme was on his dignity as a Curator; he was not prepared to accept what he considered to be impertinence from a mere Conservator, especially when that Conservator happened to be Dr Knox. He actually summoned a meeting of the Committee to receive his complaint, which he had put into writing, of Dr Knox's "incivility." The result was that the Committee decided to "admonish" Dr Knox "to avoid such conduct in future as being likely to produce consequences unpleasant in themselves and injurious to the interests of the museum." Professor Russell and Dr Gairdner were deputed to see that this resolution was carried into effect, after which, it was decided, the papers connected with the affair should be destroyed.

This might have been the end of this storm, but it proved to be only the beginning. Henceforward Knox was subjected to a whole series of pin-pricks by the Committee. On 22 March 1831 a full report was requested on "the *state* of the Museum of Comparative Anatomy"; the Committee also decided that there should be laid on the Table all the pathological and anatomical preparations added to the Museum in the preceding ten years.

These demands were not only tiresome but stupid. As Knox pointed out, the Surgeons possessed no Museum of Human or Comparative Anatomy before 1824, and when he took office then he found no detailed catalogue of the existing Museum of Pathological Anatomy. As for placing the additions on the Table, there had been 671 acquisitions to the Pathological Museum, apart from the Bell Collection, and he said:

> The Museum of Human and Comparative Anatomy made by Dr Knox contains about 546 preparations which have been collected gradually since 1st September 1824, to the present day, and mostly at his own expense.

He considered the *state* of the collections of Comparative Anatomy to be "excellent," despite the "extremely inconvenient apartments" in which some of them were housed.

It was heartless of the Surgeons to harry Dr Knox in this manner at this particular time; not only was he at the height of his own private misfortunes, but he was also in the throes of moving their exhibits yet again; this time from their "inconvenient apartments" to the new Surgeons' Hall, then in process of erection on the present site in Nicolson Street. Considering how often, and with what little assistance, Knox had transferred the museum from one place to another, it might have been thought that he would have been left in supreme command of this last removal. In this respect it could have been said of Knox, as of Wren, "Si monumentum requiris, circumspice," but this was not the attitude adopted towards him by the College, or at any rate by the Curators' subcommittee, which had been formed to supervise the move. Once again the Committee received a complaint about Dr Knox: he had not shown "a proper degree of willingness to meet the views of the Curators, but had, on the contrary, thrown many obstacles in their way." On being asked to give an explanation, Dr Knox frankly admitted that his views differed from those of the Curators' Committee on the best methods of removing the preparations, indeed he "saw no prospect of a cordial co-operation between them."[49] The Curators, on their side, remained adamant, and insisted that the Conservator must obey their instructions.

By the month of June the Curators had achieved their aim; Knox, for all his love for the Museum, could endure no more, and on 9 June 1831, he sent a letter to Dr Gairdner, President of the College:

> Dear Sir,
>
> I beg leave to acquaint the College, through you, that it is now my determination to carry into effect a measure I have for a long time contemplated, viz.:—the resignation of the Conservatorship of the museum of the College, and I request you will have the goodness to consider this notice as a resignation on my behalf of that office.
>
> R. Knox.

This was acknowledged by the President, who enquired whether Dr Knox's resignation was "absolute and unconditional —to take place immediately, or at the election in September." On 13 June the reply came from Dr Knox's brother Fred:

> Sir,
>
> My brother having left Town on Thursday last for the country where he will be until Friday, 17th, I, according to his instructions opened your letter to him of the 11th inst.
>
> I am aware that my brother has made arrangements for moving the Museum, and I have no doubt therefore that he intends his resignation of the office of Conservator to take place at the annual period (Michaelmas). I am also quite sure that he would make any sacrifice rather than a single preparation in the Museum should suffer—and that in the event of any delay occurring in the appointment of a successor his efforts for the preservation of the Museum shall continue until one is appointed.
>
> I may add that in consequence of the entire want of water and the danger of even moving about in the New Hall it was worse than useless to attempt any work there for a few days, and I believe it was this fact

---

[49] Creswell, *op. cit.*

that induced him to take an excursion in the hopes that something may be attempted on his return.

FRED. KNOX.

The College accepted Knox's resignation, and continued in Committee to revise the laws connected with the Museum and the office of Conservator, and here, surely spitefully—remembering Knox's week in the country—"Mr Syme moved as another Regulation that the Conservator shall not go out of Town without leave of the President of the College." Syme certainly had no compunction about hitting a man when he was down, and so it was that Dr Knox, on relinquishing his post as Conservator of the Museum of the Royal College of Surgeons of Edinburgh, received from that body no official word either of praise or of thanks for his seven years' work for them. The Minutes only record that on 12 August 1831 "Mr MacGillivray was elected Conservator," no reference being made to his predecessor.

Hurt, as he must have been by this ingratitude, no longer in a position to organise the transfer of his precious exhibits to their new home, and with more leisure than he had ever known, Dr Knox may have been glad of the diversion which offered itself six months later, when a whale was stranded at North Berwick. He and his brother Fred immediately bought this whale and set to work on it. This "big whale" was in fact a Rorqual (Whalebone Whale) named by them the "Great Northern Whale," it was 78 feet long and weighed 28 tons, and it took three years to prepare the skeleton, which can now be seen in the Royal Scottish Museum.

Dr Knox, working with his brother Fred, did a tremendous amount of research on it, of which a complete description is given in a fifty-nine page *Catalogue of Anatomical Preparations illustrative of the Whale*, edited by Fred. J. Knox and published in 1838. The brothers Knox spared no pains in making these preparations, and others from Greenland whales and seals, etc., to be compared with them. Dr Knox was most meticulous in the care with which he made his dissections and preparations, and it is a pity that many of these have disappeared, although thanks to the good offices of Professor Goodsir, many have been preserved in the Anatomical Museum of the University of Edinburgh. In 1833 Dr Knox read a paper to the Royal Society of Edinburgh on his Great Northern Whale, and in the following year he read another paper on his dissection of another smaller whale, the "Young Rorqual," which had been washed ashore at Queensferry, in the Firth of Forth, and which, he considered, showed most clearly the use of the "whalebone" as a filter for the collection of small fish as food.

Considering the immense amount of work which Knox did on the knotty problems of the teeth and food of whales, it is to be regretted that he never wrote his projected *History of the Cetacea*. It was perhaps a weakness of his that, with his far-ranging mind, he was apt to dissipate his energies over too wide a field, but in any case he was, in these years, still handling an enormous class.

Knox had never failed to take a lecture, even when the mob was swarming round Surgeons' Square. Now he continued his courses as though Burke and Hare had never existed. Indeed, it looked as though enthusiasm could hardly run higher than it did in 1831 when, during an outbreak of cholera in the city, Knox's rooms contained no other "subjects" than the victims of the disease, which the dissectors received with delight. The cause of cholera was then unknown, but Knox suspected flies of being in some way responsible (*v. Lancet* 1853, II). He went out on a Sunday morning (his only free day) to visit Fisherrow, near Edinburgh, where the first case had appeared, and he described the conditions he found there:

> In the village all was quiet as death. . . . On entering the cottages I found the people in great alarm. They were abandoning the sick and dying. By handling them freely, raising them up, and offering them any assistance in my power, I partly convinced the people that there existed no danger from contagion. . . . My advice to my class was very simple. Remain where you are; avoid all excess; dine on a little animal food and a glass of port wine; have no fear; with opium and warmth you may in general arrest any diarrhoea; but should a case of disease originate in the house in which you reside, leave it on the instant. I do not recollect of any student having died of the disease.

In 1829 Knox appointed as demonstrator his senior student William Fergusson, then only twenty-one. Fergusson, who had been deeply implicated in the Burke and Hare affair, never wavered in his devotion to his master. He was a most efficient dissector—learning the violin in order to make his fingers supple—and his demonstrations (to small sections of the class seated round a table) of special dissections of the different surgical regions of the body "to illustrate the operations most frequently performed" were a deservedly popular innovation.

Some years later Dr Knox took Fergusson and another of his pupils, Dr John Reid, into partnership with him for the practical class, and in 1832, when the Surgeons moved into their new Hall, he rented Old Surgeons' Hall, dilapidated as it was, because it had more accommodation than No. 10 Surgeons' Square. It looked then as though, in spite of his detractors, he might yet weather the storm, a false hope as events were soon to prove. But even if the years were to rob him of his anatomical school, of 10 Surgeons' Square, and of Old Surgeons' Hall, Dr Knox did at least enjoy the satisfaction of seeing British anatomists freed for ever from dependence on the Resurrection men. As he had always hoped it would, good did come out of evil: in August 1832 the Anatomy Act reached the Statute Book, although it had required yet another murder to get it there.

Since the Select Committee's Report in 1828, successive Governments, naturally much more interested in the passing of the Reform Bill, had paid little attention to the woes of anatomists—much disliked members of the community in any case, to whom any show of favour might prove costly in votes. However, in March 1829, Mr Warburton, M.P. for Bridport (who had been Chairman of the Select Committee) introduced a "Bill for preventing the unlawful disinterment of human bodies, and for regulating Schools of Anatomy." It was not a very good Bill, and perhaps it was as well that it was thrown out by the Lords; in 1830 Lord Calthorpe promised to re-introduce it, but a General Election was imminent, and as the *Lancet*, allowing itself one of its rare jokes, said: "Dissolution has so many horrors, that a discussion on the *subject* at the present time would be by no means agreeable." Postponement might have gone on indefinitely had there not occurred in London in 1831 "a crime of a most diabolical character, which created a sensation equal to that raised in Scotland by the atrocities of Burke and Hare."

On 5 November 1831, two men, Bishop and Williams, offered

the body of a boy of fourteen to the porter at King's College dissecting-room, who at once suspected foul play. He called the Demonstrator in Anatomy who kept the men in conversation until the police arrived and took them into custody. At the coroner's inquest the verdict was "wilful murder against some person or persons unknown" and Bishop and Williams were later tried at the Old Bailey, found guilty and hanged. Their victim was an Italian boy who earned his living by showing white mice; they had lured him to their rooms where they drugged him with opium, and then lowered him into a well, where he died of suffocation—a fate almost worse than "burking."

After this, public anger rose to such a pitch against both Resurrection men and anatomists that it was obvious that even the most lethargic Government would have to introduce some legislation, unless the whole future of British surgery was to be jeopardised. Action was quickly taken, but the Council of the Royal College of Surgeons of England moved even more quickly, when on 10 December 1831, they addressed a letter to Lord Melbourne in which they made their points succinctly. They repeated yet again the irrefutable argument that the law was gravely at fault when a medical student could be held "guilty of a misdemeanor" when trying to obtain the anatomical knowledge without which he might later, through error in practice, find himself "liable to a civil action." They reported that never had they been confronted with such difficulties; if they continued to make Practical Anatomy an obligatory examination subject for their students, it was only too likely that recent crimes would be repeated—"the large prices given for Anatomical Subjects have acted as a premium for murder." They gave the warning:

> Attention and constant suspicion on the part of the Teachers may effect much, but not all that is requisite. It is vain to imagine it always possible to distinguish the body of a person who has been murdered from that of one who has died a natural death.

They pointed out the very different methods which were employed abroad, and expressed the hope that the Legislature would devise some plan to remedy the situation:

> Whether Anatomy be taught legally or illegally, or not at all, does not concern the existing race of Practitioners in Medicine or Surgery who

have completed the period of their education; but it deeply concerns the Public.

Within a week, on 15 December 1831, Mr Warburton again introduced into the Commons a "Bill for regulating Schools of Anatomy," a Bill which was better and braver than the first. It brought British practice into line with the Continental by making it essential that everyone—student and teacher—who practised dissection should possess an official licence. It gave permission for bodies (forty-eight hours after death) to be given up for dissection by executors "or other persons having lawful possession," which, of course, included the governors of hospitals and work-houses. Twenty-four hours' notice had to be given to an official, the Inspector of Anatomy, that such removal was intended, a proper medical certificate had to be signed before the body could be moved, and after six weeks a certificate had to be sent to the Inspector that the body had been buried in consecrated ground.

The Bill had no penalties for exhumation. Mr Warburton had evidently faith in the eminent men who had given evidence before him whose opinion it was that if it were made legally possible to obtain the bodies of the unclaimed dead in the public institutions and hospitals, then the supply of "subjects" for the students would be so much greater than the demand that the Resurrection men would automatically disappear—which in fact they did.

The Committee had given considerable thought to the desirability of repealing the existing law whereby anatomists were legally entitled to receive the bodies of murderers. It was thought that this tended to connect the crime of murder in the public mind with that of the practice of dissection, and often to cast "an imputation on the character of the deceased," if later dissected. The new Bill decreed that in future, after execution, the bodies of the murderers should be either "hung in Chains, or buried within the Precincts of the Prison," but not dissected.

This time the Bill had a fairly easy passage through both Houses, and received the royal assent on 1 August 1832. It was indeed the Surgeons' Charter, without which it is difficult to imagine what the state of medical science might have been in Britain today.

The passing of the Anatomy Act in many ways marks the climax of Robert Knox's career. It was an achievement in which he had shared; as a lecturer he had done as much as anyone to emphasise the supreme importance of the study of Anatomy, as the head of an anatomical school the misfortunes which had pursued him had revealed to the world the existence of the legal shackles which bound the anatomical teachers. Dr Knox might congratulate himself on the part he had played in the long drawn-out fight for liberty in the exercise of his art; it was certain that no one else in Edinburgh would do so.

12

By 1830 Knox had become an "angry young man." He, not unnaturally, began to feel that every man's hand was against him, and his character seemed to change almost overnight. Gone was the genial host, the man who made friends so easily: the new and embittered Knox had venom on his tongue, and his wit had a cruel sarcasm that it had not had before. One writer, A. S. Currie (whose respect for Knox led him to entitle a paper for the Royal Society of Medicine, "Robert Knox, Anatomist, Scientist and Martyr") said that in his opinion Knox was by nature a courteous and amiable man who turned "cynic and satirist" as a result of the "malicious persecution of deliberate misrepresentation" from which he had suffered. He was still under forty, and henceforth he pulled no punches when he belaboured those whom he believed to be his enemies.

Towards his students Knox's attitude never changed; as always he showed to his class that high respect for which he was noted, giving them of his best, but in his lectures he now had no hesitation in attacking the fellow surgeons with whom he disagreed, or whom he considered to have betrayed him. There are, for example, his comments on John Lizars' rival School of Anatomy, where instruction was given, not from actual specimens, but from crudely drawn and brightly coloured diagrams covering the walls of the class-room. Knox described them bluntly as "huge misrepresentations of nature," and when speaking of the human heart, he would say:

"Study this beautiful piece of mechanism *in situ* . . . do not look for its anatomy upon the walls of a class-room glaring with reds and yellows and blues, such as exist in a sister institution, where the human heart and aorta are depicted as large as the whale's." [50]

In 1831 when Knox heard that Dr John Thomson had been appointed to the newly founded Chair of Pathology at Edinburgh, he scornfully referred to him as "the old chair-maker," though there was a certain wit in this remark which made it pardonable, since Thomson had already been the first Professor of Surgery to the Royal College of Surgeons of Edinburgh and the first Professor of Military Surgery in the University.

Modern minds find less excusable Knox's attack on Liston when he drew the attention of his class to a fatal mistake made by Liston a few hours earlier, when operating at the Infirmary on an aneurism of the neck. Liston was a very brilliant surgeon—he took only two minutes, "or at most three," to extract a stone from the bladder—and Knox himself on another occasion praised his "original genius and unrivalled dexterity." Now he did not refer to Liston by name, but he made his meaning all too clear by ironically referring to "the first surgeon in Europe . . . this professional celebrity . . . who among other things plumes himself upon the wonderful strength of his hands and arms, without pretension to head."

Today we may think that this was going a little too far, but it is unwise to judge nineteenth-century practice by twentieth-century standards, and Edinburgh had a long history of un-inhibited medical quarrels. In the last years of the eighteenth century Dr Gregory and John Bell had engaged in a long and fierce vendetta. Not content with affixing anti-Bell placards to the gates of the College, the Infirmary, and even to the door of the lecture-room, Dr Gregory dared to write: "Any man, if he himself or his family were sick, should as soon think of calling in a mad dog, as Mr John Bell," to which Bell retaliated by writing a book which has been described as "an octavo volume

[50] Lonsdale, *op. cit.*, p. 153.

of over 650 pages of sustained vituperation." Dr Gregory also caned the Professor of Midwifery, Dr Hamilton, for an "unguarded impertinence in print," and when he was fined £100 for assault and battery, remarked that he would gladly pay the sum a second time if he were given a chance of repeating his offence. So Dr Knox's attacks on his medical colleagues were quite in the Edinburgh tradition.

As Knox continued to give his lectures, so he continued to attend the meetings of the scientific societies where, obviously, he was no longer *persona grata*. There was one stormy meeting of the Royal Society of Edinburgh when a certain Mr John Stark, a printer in the city and a naturalist—scientifically of no professional eminence—was billed to read a paper "A Reply to Dr Knox's Essay on the Food of the Herring and Salmon," and as the result of a rumour that it would "contain an exposure of Dr Knox's plagiarism and recklessness of statement"—the second accusation of the kind to be levelled against Knox—the Hall was crowded to capacity. As Dr Knox's favourite recreation was angling, and as he had done considerable research on the food of the fish in question, and was, above all a, scientist to whom accuracy of statement was of the highest importance, he listened with mounting impatience to Mr Stark's lecture. For once he lost his temper; at the end he rose and spoke his mind:

> "Is it necessary for me, the friend and companion of Baron Cuvier, to defend myself in the society of my compeers against the base and personal scurrilities of a mere dabbler in science?" [51]

He referred to Stark as the "catspaw" of the "professorial clique" who were working against him: one of the professors whom he actually named being Professor Christison. Knox did not on this occasion mention Syme, although Syme was present, and shot at him a barbed question about whales, which he deflected without difficulty. Meetings of Edinburgh scientific societies did not usually end in uproar, so perhaps it is not surprising that after this Dr Knox came to be less in demand as a speaker.

Knox was gradually losing the things which made life agreeable, but the wolf was as yet far from his door. Then, suddenly,

[51] Lonsdale, *op. cit.*, p. 191.

about the year 1834, he had to face the fact that his annual income was slowly, but steadily, decreasing, as the number of pupils attending his classes grew smaller. Knox attributed this to the decline in the number of medical students coming to study at Edinburgh, for which he blamed the University authorities and he was thought to be the anonymous author of a pamphlet, "An Examination into the Causes of the Declining Reputation of the Medical Faculty in the University of Edinburgh," published in 1834. Although new medical schools were springing up, and Edinburgh was facing more competition than in 1826 (the peak year when there were 900 medical students) there was a large degree of truth in Knox's allegation.

The main problem confronting the University was the method of teaching Surgery, which had been a point at issue since the end of the eighteenth century when Alexander Monro, *secundus*, selfishly opposed the foundation of a separate Chair of Surgery in the University, simply because he and his father had always taught Surgery as well as Anatomy. Unfortunately his son Alexander Monro, *tertius*, persisted in this attitude, and as late, as 1829, protested against the Royal Commission's suggestion that the separate Chair should be instituted. The Town Council, the patrons of the University—originally founded, it must be remembered, under Charter of James VI, as the Town's College— felt that, for the general good, Monro must in some fashion be circumvented, and approached the Government to this end, supported by Dr John Thomson, who addressed a memorial to Lord Melbourne on the benefits which would accrue to the University by the foundation of a Chair of Pathology. The result was that in 1831, with very little warning, two Regius Professorships, one of Pathology and one of Surgery, were established; the professors nominated being, respectively, perhaps by no coincidence, Dr John Thomson and his former assistant, Mr John W. Turner.

The Senatus of the University was furious at this intervention by the Crown and protested to Lord Melbourne, who replied, in effect, that what was done could not be undone. The Surgeons of Edinburgh—although their College had had its own Professor of Surgery since 1804, who in 1831 was the now translated

Turner—were also furious. The new professors were both Whigs, and Dr Knox and ten other Edinburgh lecturers, all members of the College, made their views on the appointments quite clear when, in 1832, they signed a petition to the House of Commons on the subject. The petitioners did not mince matters, they said that they were prepared to prove that the recent appointments, which were in the gift of the Crown,

> took place in a hurried and clandestine manner, thereby preventing the claims of other members of the profession from being duly considered; and it is the general belief of the profession that the Chairs were bestowed more as the reward of political than of medical zeal.

They prayed that the Honourable House would:

> take such measures as to prevent improper appointments in future . . . and take measures to prevent the interests of medicine and science being sacrificed to political intrigue.

Knox was always fighting for the recognition of merit and the suppression of chicanery, and here he had a good case. Strange things had also happened in the past, when nepotism had governed the University's choice of candidates for professorial posts, and Town Councillors, very often completely ignorant of medical affairs, were the final arbiters. Now the Government had come in, and made the confusion worse. Not only had the appointments a political flavour, but attendance at the new professors' lectures was made a compulsory qualification for the M.D. degree, and this Knox considered to be a shocking state of affairs; it put an undue strain on the student, and also on his purse. Furthermore it tended to have a bad effect on the professors, who knew that they would always have full classes, whether their efforts warranted them or not. Knox was probably right about this, but it was not the kind of statement which would win him friends within the University. The introduction of compulsory courses hit him and all the extra-mural lecturers very hard; the more lectures the student had to attend within the University, the less time and less money he had to seek instruction elsewhere, and Knox thought that the large number of private lecturers in Edinburgh was a proof that the University teaching was unsatisfactory. Knox was, in the main, right in these matters, as indeed he so often was, but the mere fact of being right is no passport to success, nor to popularity.

Knox himself had, so far, never been a candidate for any Chair, but in 1837—suffering, perhaps, some financial embarrassment, (for he had a wife and five children to support) or wishing, perhaps, to reassert his status—he applied for this very Chair of Pathology, just vacated by Dr John Thomson.

Knox's letter of application to the Lord Provost and Town Council had to be written in haste. For some unexplained reason, it was not until the afternoon of 6 July 1837, that he heard of Thomson's actual resignation, and he was further informed that the Council intended to hold a meeting at 10 a.m. on the following day to elect his successor. Knox had little time to lose, and his letter is short and to the point. He detailed his qualifications: his experience as an Army surgeon at home and abroad, his medical studies in Paris, his museum work, his numerous publications, and not least, his anatomical teaching—his classes "probably exceeding in numbers those taught by any individual in Britain." With not a little pride, he enclosed the letter he had received two years earlier from the French Academy of Medicine, informing him that he had been elected a Corresponding Member, an honour he explained, "bestowed on few foreigners." One which proved that in Paris, at any rate, his reputation had remained untarnished by his unfortunate connexion with Burke and Hare.

Perhaps Knox was a little ill-advised to make it clear in the last paragraph of his letter that, although he was applying for the Chair, he was unrepentant about having referred to its establishment as "a political job of the very worst description." He also stated his belief that the medical student was entitled to obtain his education "where and how he likes," therefore to render attendance at any lectures compulsory, created a "scandalous monopoly," most harmful and unfair to the extra-mural lecturers, and altogether pernicious. Yet Knox did add, rather charmingly, that if he had the good fortune to be selected, "those energies and activity hitherto employed in a fair and honourable rivalry to the University, will then be devoted to its support."

Knox's hopes were running high, but the Town Council did

not meet on 7 July as he had expected to elect the new Professor. On that day, the very day after Dr Knox's application—surely a strange coincidence—they received, and had to consider, a joint proposal from Professor Alison, Professor Christison, Sir Charles Bell, and Professor James Syme, that the Chair of Pathology, being "not required or expedient," should be abolished. In which case, they said, they would be prepared to deliver a course of lectures on General Pathology, the proceeds of which would meet the retiring allowance of £150 payable to Dr Thomson by his successor. It may be that they were acting in good faith, but James Syme was a signatory and so was Christison, and Charles Bell had only recently returned to Edinburgh, and possibly was not yet cognisant of all the ramifications of University politics. In these circumstances it seems legitimate to wonder if their convictions would have been quite as "thorough" as they proclaimed them to be if Dr Knox had not, at the eleventh hour, presented himself as a candidate for the Chair.

Dr Knox, not without reason, was very angry; on 15 July he addressed another letter to the Lord Provost and Town Council:

> I beg leave respectfully again to offer myself as a Candidate for the Pathological Chair, and to obtrude myself on your notice by a Second Letter, for which I plead in excuse the necessity of rendering my former proposal clear and distinct, and to reply to a communication you have in the interval received from a junto of the Professors of the University.

It was a surprising move, unworthy, Knox thought, "of the known characters for candour and plain-dealing of Dr Alison and Sir Charles Bell"—by implication, worthy of the other two signatories whom he did not name, Christison and Syme. Knox pointed out that as Bell, Alison, and Syme held diametrically opposing views on medical and surgical methods, and as Christison, a chemist, had "all the advantages of a great previous ignorance," it would be extremely difficult for the four of them to give a joint course of lectures without contradicting one another and causing confusion in the minds of their hearers. On the whole, however, Knox kept his temper and restrained his pen in this second letter, and confined himself to restating his arguments against compulsory lectures.

Soon the whole of Edinburgh was in a furore over this question of the future of the Chair of Pathology, and the Town Council was inundated with letters, as professors and others rushed into print. It need hardly be said that Knox was not appointed, and the solution found to the problem was probably the most sensible: the *status quo* continued to exist for another five years. The Chair of Pathology was not abolished, and Dr John Thomson, though in ill-health and well over seventy, continued to hold it until 1842, his successor then being William Henderson, who later on, surprised and pained his supporters by becoming a homoeopath.

Knox's next step was to apply for the post of Lecturer in Anatomy to the art students of the Scottish Academy, a position for which he would seem to have been admirably suited, having acquired a sound knowledge of Art during his student days in Paris. He was not appointed. "Poor Knox," said Sir Thomas Dick Lauder, "had not a vote."

In the same year, no whit deterred by his increasing un-popularity, Knox applied for the Chair of Physiology about to be vacated by Professor Alison, but the odds against him were greater than they had been when he applied for the Chair of Pathology. By 1841 Edinburgh had realised that Dr Knox, the employer of Burke and Hare, was not only politically a "radical," a dangerous thing to be in the aftermath of the Reform Bill, when Britain was highly nervous of "left" opinion; but he was also an unbeliever, a member of no recognised church, an "atheist" and an "infidel."

It is difficult to discover Robert Knox's views on religion: often he seems to have more in common with twentieth-century Humanism than with nineteenth-century Presbyterianism. It is true that the books he kept on his dressing-room table were *Don Quixote* and the *Bible*, but he refused to be bound by the dogma of any organised religion. Lonsdale was puzzled by this side of his hero's character. He knew Knox intimately, and believed him to be a man "of high reverence and belief," though without any "outward religious manifestations"; but he was obviously worried by the doctor's diatribes against the "idolatrous credulity and ignorance" of religious sects, and his belief, so very different from that of the good folk of Edinburgh, that through the ages national churches were but the instruments of "governmental and priestly tyrannies." Nor could Lonsdale fully comprehend either Knox's compassion for man's "finiteness" and failure to fathom the mystery of life or his transcending faith in a science that one day would reveal "the great Creative scheme."

Some ten years later Knox wrote of religious persecution and bigotry as follows:

> Under an Augustus or an Antonine, man was free to worship the deity of his choice, or of his belief,—to practise whatever religious folly he preferred: throughout Europe at the present time to cease to be orthodox—to cease to conform—is to forfeit all or most of the privileges of citizenship.[52]

Meanwhile he did nothing to conceal his shocking opinions from his fellow citizens:

> Christian Mission to the followers of Islam! To benefit or destroy? Mahometanism has its book, that does not require to be elaborated by millions of sermons. Mahometanism is peaceful, sober and virtuous. Can this be said of the denizens of British cities? [53]

> Are we to be told that the Kaffir of this cerebral stamp [showing a cranium during a lecture] is a savage because he lives in the " wilde," and that John Bull is the happy creature of civilization because he wears breeches, learns catechisms, and does his best to cheat his neighbours—always, of course, on Christian principles! [54]

Statements such as these had their repercussions. The Town Council had not forgotten that under King James VI's Charter they ruled their College "with the advice" of the Ministers of the Kirk, so it was not surprising that when Dr Knox called on Mr Adam Black, the well-known publisher, in the hope of winning his vote,

> Mr Black observed: "Of your remarkable abilities, Doctor, and your fitness for the Chair I have no doubt; but you know that our Town Council have strong religious scruples."
> "Well," replied Knox, "am I not as good a Christian as Baillie ——, or any of my neighbours?" "It may be," said the publisher, "had you only

---

[52] *Races of Men*, 2nd edn., p. 555.
[53] Lonsdale, *op. cit.*, p. 324.
[54] Lonsdale, *op. cit.*, p. 149.

PLATE 6

William Burke in the condemned cell. "Drawn from Life in the Lock-up House on the day before his Execution by his own consent," by Benjamin W. Crombie.

From *Noxiana*, by courtesy of the Trustees of the National Library of Scotland.

been an Elder of the Kirk, Doctor!" "Ah, ah, I see," rejoined Knox, "the Calvinistic credentials are wanting."[55]

It seems likely that by this time Knox had no delusions about his chances of becoming a Professor, and in his application for the Chair of Physiology, was only entering the lists in order to air his views by getting them into print. This letter to the Lord Provost and Town Council is very different from his former direct and dignified application for the Chair of Pathology; it is diffuse and satirical, and contains personal attacks on the other candidates. He mentions in it "a natural disposition of speaking aloud what I think, reckless of results." Here he had no desire to curb that disposition, and he was outspoken in his condemnation of the University: the very style in which he sets forth his qualifications is both arrogant and sarcastic:

> My successful teaching; the confidence of thousands of medical men; of the many hundreds I have taught, including a very large majority of the distinguished rising talent of the age; the Museum I have formed, these, my Lord, surely furnish the best, I had almost said the only, sure evidence of zeal, industry and ability, terms much used by the Council of late in respect to Candidates for Chairs, but to which no very precise meaning seems occasionally to be attached. . . .
>
> I have maintained a fair average number of students against the most determined opposition, an opposition including not merely the rivalry of numerous talented men, but the bitter hostility of the University, and of most members of the Council of the City. . . .
>
> Of my ultimate success, as a Lecturer within the University walls, neither your Lordship nor any of the Council, can have even a shadow of doubt.

The shrinking attendance at his classes must have been a cause of great anxiety to Knox, for the situation was far worse than it had been in 1837; now, four years later, the total number of medical students in Edinburgh was no more than 356. Knox put the blame for this decline fairly and squarely on the University, and for three reasons: the overloading of the curriculum, the monopoly which Edinburgh University exercised "with baneful effects," the absence from the University "of all men of originality, and of European reputation." Nor did Knox think that the

[55] Lonsdale, *op. cit.*, p. 264.

election of any of his rivals for the Chair would remedy this last defect:

> Nothing throughout this whole business has surprised me so much as the strict resemblance between the three Candidates; their repeated and extraordinary failures, their bolstered up reputations; their total want of all originality; their unpopularity with the student or the taught; their powers of mystifying the plainest facts.

Of the three candidates Knox poured the most ridicule on Allen Thomson, son of Dr John Thomson. He described how, backed by his relatives and the Town Council, this young man had embarked as a lecturer on three unsuccessful courses on Physiology, then he was "pensioned on a noble English Duke," and thereafter a "Chair was created for him in a Northern University." Knox asked:

> Will your Lordship venture to elect this person (who is notwithstanding a most industrious and painstaking Physiologist, although a most deplorably unpopular Lecturer) in the face of such a failure?

The answer was in the affirmative. It was Allen Thomson who was appointed Professor of Physiology. In the various medical histories Thomson's career is not reported quite as Knox reported it—he was, indeed, a pioneer in microscopic anatomy—but the facts are not to be disputed: Thomson had been an extra-mural lecturer in Edinburgh, private physician to the Duke of Bedford, and Professor of Anatomy at Marischal College, Aberdeen. He held the Chair of Physiology at Edinburgh until 1848, when he went to Glasgow as Professor of Anatomy.

Knox never applied for another Chair in the University of Edinburgh.

During the year 1841 Knox had suffered many tribulations, but the last and most terrible blow was still in store. Before the year ended he was to lose his wife, who died of puerperal fever, following the birth of her sixth child. Lonsdale has well described the grief and emotion with which Knox told him of her death:

> The effort to appear gracious as he approached could not be sustained; his face and eyes betrayed what he had passed through, and all he could say, on clasping my hands in his own, was—"She is gone, she is gone. . . .".

> Poor Knox, though wanting in many things, was sound to the core,
> when love and affection stood face to face with the sufferings of mortality

He had need of all his philosophy when, early in the New Year, his little son, John, aged four, contracted scarlet fever and swiftly followed his mother to the grave.

13

In his last letter to the Lord Provost and Town Council, Knox had said that, if the decline of the University were to continue:

> the most prudent course would be to follow rapidly the steps of the Listons and the Fergussons, the Turners and Grahams, and Reids, and seek in the metropolis of the Empire, that return for exertion and hard-earned reputation denied us here.

Some people must have believed that Knox, too, intended to set off for London, but he put an end to such rumours by inserting a notice in the *London Medical Gazette* for 2 July 1841, which stated that "Dr Knox has not, and never had, any intention of removing from Edinburgh."

Knox was an Edinburgh man by birth and education, and it is evident that he would not willingly have left his native city had circumstances not been too much for him. But the world that he had known was disintegrating; not only was he rejected by the University, but his ever-diminishing classes made him reconsider his position at Surgeons' Square. Fergusson and Reid had left him to take up independent appointments, and his brother Fred had gone to New Zealand, so he took into partnership his former student and future biographer, Henry Lonsdale, and accepted the invitation of another extra-mural body, the Argyle Square Medical School, to become their lecturer in Anatomy. He later recommended his own lectures on Anatomy and Physiology, and then suffered the most humiliating rebuff of his career, when he found that for neither course could he, Knox "primus et incomparabilis," attract a class.

By the end of 1842, at the age of forty-nine, even Dr Knox had to admit that Edinburgh had cast him out. No alternative was left; he must accept the verdict and go. Whether, in retrospect,

Edinburgh has reason for self-congratulation is doubtful. Surely, when weighed in the balance, Dr Knox's merits were greater than his faults; arrogant, radical, egotistical, and free-thinking he may have been, and unwise in his dealings with Burke and Hare, yet he was one of the greatest lecturers and teachers that Edinburgh has ever known, and the mainspring of his every action was devotion to the cause he had at heart—the advancement of anatomical science, especially in the Medical School of Edinburgh. That this Medical School, which Knox had seen to be in decline, did in fact recover and come to a fine flowering with Lister, was due in no small part to the instruction in anatomy given by Knox to his pupil surgeons in Surgeons' Square. To one of these pupils in particular, John Goodsir, the University of Edinburgh was particularly indebted; he became Professor of Anatomy in 1846, when Monro, *tertius*, did at last retire, and believing what his master, Knox, had taught him, that "a piece of true dissection ought to turn out an object of wonder and beauty," he soon had injected sufficient new life into the course to collect a class of over 300 students. This may have been some small crumb of comfort for Knox, but probably not very much, as by then, he, without whose teaching British surgery might not have progressed as it did in the nineteenth century, was struggling for bare existence.

When he had at last decided to leave Edinburgh, Knox placed his family in charge of his nephew, with his daughter, Mary, aged seventeen, as housekeeper, and then he took the road to the south. He travelled by easy stages, staying with some of his old students on the way, but when he reached London he found no welcoming hand. None of the anatomists of the metropolis had any greeting for him, nor any intention of allowing him to join their ranks as a lecturer. The London surgeons were only too thankful that the scandal, when it came, should have occurred in Edinburgh, not London, and that the odium should have fallen on Knox and not on them, although they had been more heavily involved with the Resurrectionists than he. It has been truly said of him that he was "hounded out of society to wander up and down the country for years," to become, in truth, the "surgeons' scapegoat."[56]

[56] C. H. Turner, *The Inhumanists.* London 1932.

In London he was lonely and sad:

> listlessly pacing London's idle busy streets, with nothing to look at but miles of hideous brick walls, with holes in them called doors and windows.[57]

Not only was this abhorrent to him, but it is easy to see from his letters how much he missed his children. He sent money for them to his nephew:

> Do not forget to make all round you comfortable. Mary, I suppose, manages chiefly; let bonny Bre and Bob have some pocket-money for sweets.

On another occasion, when he was lecturing in Essex, Knox wrote:

> You cannot think what pleasure I have in making you all comfortable. I do believe that were it not for this pleasure I would not take the trouble to take another meal; for I am tired of the world, its humbug and common-place. . . . The morning is, as usual, misty, cold, rainy, dark; and I hear the east winds singing mournfully through the crevices of my bed-room. Let us fly to finer climates, where we may at least see the sun.[58]

But this was not to be. In order to earn some sort of income Knox travelled round the country on a series of lecture tours— going by what he called "the most frightful and most odious of all means of conveyance, the rail"—and he wrote for more and more medical journals.

Knox had always had a facile pen, and as a young man had written many articles for one of the earliest of medical magazines, the *Edinburgh Medical and Surgical Journal*. Then, immediately after the Burke and Hare affair, perhaps to take his mind off the horrors which haunted him, he had produced two translations from the French, Cloquet's *System of Human Anatomy* in 1829, and Beclard's *General Anatomy* in 1830, which were invaluable to all British anatomists. There was a great scarcity of English textbooks; when Barclay began to teach Anatomy he had only one for his students, and that was the *London Dissector*. For many years Comparative Anatomy could only be studied by means of French books and plates, and here, of course, Knox's knowledge of the language gave him a flying start. So it is not

[57] *Fish and Fishing in the Lone Glens of Scotland*, p. 11.
[58] Lonsdale, *op. cit.*, p. 377.

surprising that in the anxious days of 1839 Knox returned to this field with a translation for the *Lancet* of De Blainville's lectures on Comparative Osteology, lectures which he had actually attended in Paris.

He was a prolific writer—in the hungry eighteen-forties he had need to be—and if the papers contributed by him to medical journals should ever be collected, they will occupy volumes. It was fortunate for him that he was a man matched with the hour, and that an expanding new market existed for his pen; medical journalism in London was a recent development, and he was one of the pioneers. The *Lancet*, founded in 1823, was quickly followed by the *London Medical Gazette*, the *Medical Press*, etc., and Knox contributed to them all on a wide variety of subjects, ranging from human anatomy and physiology to an "Inquiry into the Present State of our Knowledge respecting the Orang-Outang and Chimpanzee," and the "Nostrils of the Horse," reprinted in the *Medical Times* from the *Veterinary Record*.

Knox must have relied entirely on journalism and lecturing for an income during these years. He scorned to commercialise his scientific knowledge, and bemoaned the attitude towards science adopted by contemporary industrial England. His interest lay in pure, not applied, science. As he wrote sadly, or perhaps proudly:

> The desire to discover the unknown, in the interests of science only, without any reference to a practical bearing, is a rare quality of the human mind.[59]

In order to keep body and soul together, Knox soon had to embark upon his most ambitious series of lecture tours, which took him to such cities as Newcastle, Manchester, and Birmingham, and the subject which he chose for these lectures (later published in book form) was "Races of Men." Knox had early appreciated the importance of racial differences, when in his twenty-first year, he had spent a holiday in the Scottish Highlands, and meeting Highlanders for the first time, had realised how very different these Celts were from the Lowland Scots with whom he had spent his boyhood. Naturally contact with the

[59] *Fish and Fishing in the Lone Glens of Scotland*, p. 136.

black races of the Cape, when he was on military service, increased his interest in ethnology, and it remained with him all his life, so it is not surprising that he should have chosen such a subject for these public lectures. It also had the merit of being sufficiently elastic to enable him to discuss almost any topic of current interest, which he did to some purpose, with many sarcastic gibes at the English and their Government.

Some of Knox's Cassandra-like prophecies, founded on his knowledge of the negro and of English colonialism can still strike home. He is, for instance, particularly interesting on the subject of Central and South Africa:

> I incline then to the opinion that the dark races may for many ages hold the tropical regions; that many countries now in the military occupation of the fair races may and will revert to the dark; that it would be a better policy, perhaps, to teach them artificial wants and the habits and usages of civilization. Commerce alone, I think, can reach Central Africa; the Negro must be taught the value of his labour.[60]

He had no delusions about the racial problem at the Cape:

> The Dutch at the Cape have a perfect horror for the coloured races; it extends to the Mulatto, whom they absolutely despise. The placing a coloured man in an important official situation in South Africa, has caused to Britain the loss of some millions, and laid the basis for the ultimate separation of that colony from Britain.[61]

Dr Knox added: "No one seems much to care for the dark races."[62] Of India he said:

> Neither Celt nor Saxon can labour in a tropical country, they may seize a country, as we have done India, and hold it by the bayonet as we do that vast territory; but we cannot colonize it; it is no part of Britain in any sense, and never will be; the white race can never till the fields of Hindustan. . . . If we are to hold India, it can only be as military masters lording it over a slave population.[63]

On the whole, it is difficult today to understand what made these lectures so popular with Knox's contemporaries. Perhaps the taste of the present generation for harangues on Race has been sated by two German wars; perhaps the lecturer, with his

[60] *Races of Men*, p. 312.　　[61] *Op. cit.*, p. 473, n. 7.
[62] *Op. cit.*, p. 314.　　[63] *Op. cit.*, p. 264.

charm and expertise, could bring to life what in cold print seem very dry bones indeed. There is no denying the fact that the book *Races of Men*, published in 1850, is heavy going for the reader, and it is all too obvious that this kind of thing was not Knox's forte.

The *Lancet* critic, reviewing the book, damned with faint praise: "the work of Dr Knox cannot be altogether shelved, in the present transition state of ethnological science." Twelve years later, in the obituary notice of Knox in the *Medical Times*, comment was made on *Races of Men*:

> A work which his acrimony, scepticism, want of proper arrangement, carelessness and repetition would have damned, had it not been for its truth. . . . It is good that we in our day, have had a monitor in Dr Knox, pointing out that "the empire over which the sun never sets" stands not exactly by our own virtues or own will, and that, perhaps, when we have served the designs of Providence, we, too, may be ranked with the things of the past.

This last sentence is more or less a paraphrase of the final paragraph of Knox's book, which had left his readers much food for thought:

> For millions and millions of years the world rolled through space without man; his absence was not felt; he hopes his presence to be now eterne [eternal]: Creature of yesterday! Such would have been the language of the ancient saurians, could they have spoken,—"Look at our might and strength; look at the glorious world around; the vast and beauteous forms which everywhere decorate the earth. This can never come to a close." But it did, and that frequently too: from the past, judge of the future.[64]

The book reached a second edition in 1862. It is pleasant to think that its royalties helped to fill Dr Knox's depleted coffers, but it is sad to consider what might have been. Although *Races of Men* reveals facets of Knox's wide-ranging, original, and well-stocked mind, as well as his foibles, it cost hours of his time in writing the original lectures, and travelling about the country to deliver them at all the various provincial "scientific and philosophical societies" which invited him; hours which might have been put to so much better purpose had fate left him in his

[64] *Races of Men*, p. 446.

class-room at Surgeons' Square to educate his students and pursue his own research on the human frame, particularly in the field in which his early interests lay—embryology.

14

In 1844 Dr Knox came back to his native land, but having disposed of his Anatomical School in Surgeons' Square to Henry Lonsdale, he did something unusual for an Edinburgh man: he went to Glasgow. There he had obtained the post of lecturer in Anatomy at the Portland Street School, a small, but important, medical school. It was officially recognised by the examining boards, and it had a well-equipped laboratory, as well as a lecture-theatre and dissecting-room, and a staff of four. Just as Dr Barclay's extra-mural classes had attracted Knox when he was an Edinburgh student, so now the Portland Street School attracted the boy who afterwards became famous as Sir Benjamin Ward Richardson, who in his autobiography, *Vita Medica*, gives an excellent description of his experiences at this time and of his relationship with Knox.

Richardson attended Knox's course "On the Brain and Nervous System," and as the class was small, had the privilege of dissecting under his personal supervision. He described the lectures as "most brilliant," and very practical for examination purposes. He writes:

> I was personally very sorry when the course was over, as there could not have been a more perfect teacher, nor a more accomplished man than Knox. He aired none of his own sorrows, resented none of the attacks made upon him, whispered not a word about his own poverty, but did what he was paid to do, and did it well. I found that Knox's lectures were appreciated far beyond the circle to which they were delivered, for many a student who did not attend them was glad to copy from the notes of those who did, and to exchange conversation upon them. On my part I gathered no information that extended beyond the lectures. I entered into none of the heated current debates respecting the conduct of Knox, and during the course I never spoke to him on any subject except the one on which he was engaged as a teacher.

Lonsdale says that Knox's class at the Portland Street School was so small that "he returned his fees to his pupils before

November was out," whereas Richardson seems to imply that the course was ended. Possibly Knox shortened it somewhat, for he must have found daily life in Glasgow intolerable. Richardson tells how:

> If Knox were walking in a public place, one of the crowd would be likely to touch a friend and ask curiously,—"Did you ever see that man before? Have you any idea who he is?"
>
> And if his friend did not know, the questioner's reply would be,— "Why, it's Knox, the anatomist!"
>
> And then both would stare with all their eyes, and probably would turn away trying to conceal themselves quietly, as if they had seen the devil.

Soon Knox left the city and crossed the Border, thankful, for once, for the anonymity of London. He never lived in Scotland again.

Richardson mentions Knox's poverty, and there is no doubt that at this time in Glasgow he was very near the starvation line. Lonsdale tells a poignant story of an evening meeting of the Glasgow Medico-Chirurgical Society when the surgeons had been examining a terribly mutilated patient, for whom they afterwards made a collection. When the hat reached Knox, he generously slipped in a crown-piece, and then left the hall with his friend, Dr Adams. On their way home Knox went into a baker's shop and bought a penny roll and asked for a glass of water. It was only later that Dr Adams discovered that Knox had had no dinner, and had eaten nothing since breakfast but the penny roll.

Nevertheless Sir Robert Christison's statement, quite often quoted, that Knox towards the end of his life acted as "lecturer, demonstrator, or showman to a travelling party of Ojibbeway Indians" can only be a piece of wishful thinking. It is true that the Ojibbeway Indians had been the sensation of London in 1839, when they were presented to members of the Royal Family, as well as to members of the public, who were all "delighted to see and talk with these descendants of a fast-vanishing race," but there is nothing to prove that Dr Knox took anything more than a scientific interest in them, natural in the author of *Races of Men*.

But it is not to be denied that things were going very badly with Knox. He ceased to be able to pay his annual subscription to the Widows' Fund of the Royal College of Surgeons of Edinburgh, which by February 1844 was £21 10s in arrears, and by November he was being threatened by them with legal proceedings for his default. In 1848, his subscription to the Royal Society of Edinburgh having also fallen into arrears, his name was struck off its Roll of Fellows. In the following year the Royal Society took a further step, and actually expunged his name from the Roll ("election cancelled"), hardly a generous gesture towards a gifted man whom, in the days of his prosperity, they had always been glad to welcome.

Yet Knox, as Richardson had noted, "aired none of his own sorrows, resented none of the attacks made upon him," and he arouses our admiration by the manner in which, during these difficult years, he refused to succumb to self-pity or to be daunted by adversity; always he kept abreast of the times, his mind extravert and open to all the topics of the day. While he was in Glasgow he even devised a plan to enrich the city merchants. To one of them, a Mr Downie, he wrote a letter with the intriguing suggestion that a meeting of merchants should be held in Glasgow to consider an ambitious scheme for founding a colony in "extra-tropical South Africa," with a view to making it ultimately "the best wool producing country in the world."[65] The first step, he suggested, should be to form a company, "for the purchase and sale of the vast unoccupied territory," and for the introduction to it of the merino and of improved breeds of cattle. The merinos and shorthorns should be accompanied not only by a "few steady men," but also by "two or three scientific men." Knox was very insistent on this point because, from the geological formations he had observed, he suspected the existence of "gold and everything valuable," and he said:

> sailors are not the right persons to find out these things. Parry and the King's Own brought home quartz rocks from the Arctic regions which these good men mistook for marble.

Had the merchants of Glasgow adopted Knox's plan they might have made their fortune and his, for the date of his letter is 15 September 1844. Unfortunately, Knox's finances being in

[65] Letter of R. Knox. N.L.S. Ms. 2618, f. 288.

such a parlous state, he took no further steps to become a gold prospector in South Africa.

He followed minutely every movement in the medical world, and in the summer of 1845, when he was in London at the time the Physic and Surgery Bill was being debated in the House, he wrote at once, after it was "talked out," to tell Dr Adams of its fate. Knox had never approved of it; had it been passed it would have put Scots graduates, with their hard-won diplomas, at a grave disadvantage, as it envisaged the foundation of a college of general practitioners prepared to admit non-graduates. But Knox made it clear to Dr Adams that he was by no means against Government intervention in the affairs of the medical profession:

> I have reflected deeply on the state of affairs in Glasgow, Edinburgh and the North, but more especially in Glasgow, and I have come to the deliberate opinion, after having looked about me in London, that anything so low, so disgraceful, so entirely unprofessional as the state of educational establishments and of the Medical and Surgical Faculty generally, never did before exist in the world. I most solemnly declare to you, it beggars all belief, and the Legislature should be called to step in to stop it with a strong hand.[66]

The remedy for this, as far as Scotland was concerned, though delayed for thirteen years, was provided by the passing of an "Act to make provision for the better government and discipline of the Universities of Scotland, and improving and regulating the course of study therein." The year 1858 also saw the passing of "The Medical Act," which set up the General Medical Council, with authorisation to prepare a Register of qualified medical practitioners.

Dr Knox, in his letter to Dr Adams, had used strong terms in his condemnation of contemporary medical education. But one of the worst aspects, at which he only hinted, was that at this time it was common knowledge that at various centres, but most particularly in Glasgow, it was possible for a dishonest medical student to obtain forged certificates of class attendance. Little did Knox guess that within a couple of years he would find himself the victim of just such a scoundrel.

[66] " An Hitherto Unpublished Letter by Dr Robert Knox," *Glasgow Medical Journal*, 1923, c., 5.

The scandalous case of Mr John Henry Osborne, of Epperstone, in the county of Nottingham, was first brought to the notice of the public on 29 May 1847, when a letter from Mr John Edward Fosbrooke was published in the *Lancet*. In it he explained at length and in detail why the medical men of his neighbourhood had been mightily surprised when in August 1845 Osborne's name had appeared as a successful candidate for the College of Surgeons' diploma,[67] since it was well known that he had only studied Medicine for nine months, from November 1844 to the summer of 1845. Mr Fosbrooke had communicated these facts to Mr Belfour, Secretary of the College of Surgeons of England, who however, assured him that he had made enquiries of the signatories of Mr Osborne's certificates, and that their replies seemed satisfactory.

If Osborne had taken no further action all might have been well, but in August 1845 he took over his father's practice of surgeon-apothecary at Epperstone. Mr Fosbrooke, noble watch-dog that he was, at once brought to the notice of the Society of Apothecaries that Osborne was practising without their licence, and in June 1846, they issued a writ against him, which was withdrawn when he promised to sit for his examination.

The certificates of attendance at lectures which Osborne produced to prove the adequacy of his medical education were many. The majority had been obtained in Glasgow at the Andersonian and Portland Street extra-mural schools; they bore dates between 1 May 1844 and July 1845, and covered the subjects of Surgery, Practice of Medicine, Chemistry, Botany, Midwifery, and Materia Medica. He had also a certificate from Dr Buchanan of attendance at the Andersonian at his Anatomy and Physiology lectures and the accompanying demonstrations and dissections, a certificate which attested that during the period, 1 November 1844—30 April 1845, he had "carefully dissected." Perhaps this was a stock phrase, as Osborne produced a certificate similarly worded from Dr Knox, for attendance at his lectures on Anatomy and Physiology and the accompanying demonstrations and dissections at the School of Queen's College, Argyle Square, Edinburgh, from 4 November 1839—1 May 1840. Osborne

[67] Royal College of Surgeons of England.

also had a certificate from the surgeons to the Glasgow Royal Infirmary, A. J. Hannay and J. A. Lawrie, to the effect that he had attended "very regularly," from 1 November 1843 to 20 July 1845, the surgical practice of the hospital. He had also attended the clinical surgery courses at the Infirmary given by Dr Pagan and Dr Hannay. Not content with all this, Osborne had a document signed by his father, stating that he had been apprenticed to him from 1 May 1833—1 May 1838, with "extensive opportunities of witnessing medical and surgical practice, and also numerous cases of midwifery."

It was an impressive list of qualifications, all guaranteed by young Osborne to be "in every respect correct and true," but the worthy Mr Fosbrooke was not impressed. He made his own careful and far-reaching enquiries, so that, when he came to write to the *Lancet* in 1847, he had no hesitation in declaring that in this list "three distinct acts of fraud were at once manifest." First, that the indentures of Osborne's apprenticeship with his father were "antedated by at least seven years (and when he wanted one month of twelve years of age) in order that he might have a less extended curriculum"; secondly, that he had "obtained from Dr Knox a certificate constituting his first annus medicus of attendance upon anatomical lectures and of a six-months' course of dissections, with demonstrations at the Queen's College, Argyle Street, Edinburgh, during the winter session 1839-40, Mr Osborne never having been in Edinburgh at that time"; and lastly, that he had "obtained a certificate of attendance on the hospital practice of the Glasgow Royal Infirmary for one year and seven months, from Nov. 1st, 1843, to July, 1845, whereas he was only entitled to a certificate for nine months."

Mr Fosbrooke then produced proof for his allegations. For the first, the Parish Register recorded the baptism of John Henry Osborne on 4 June 1821, and his actual indentures to his father were drawn up in 1840, not 1833, as stated.

Then, following the boy's career with care, Mr Fosbrooke obtained a statement from the Rev. Mr Burder, headmaster of the Nottingham Free Grammar School, that Osborne had been a pupil at the school from 30 January 1837 until Christmas 1839, which proved that he could not have been in Edinburgh during the first half of the session of 1839-40, as certified by Dr Knox. This was corroborated by a fellow student of Osborne's at the Andersonian, who remembered that he had there competed for a first-year Anatomy prize, which he could not have done had he had any previous anatomical training. Mr Fosbrooke also applied to Dr Henry Lonsdale, to whom Dr Knox's registers had passed when he bought the School from him, and received the reply:

> I have looked carefully through the class register of students attending the practical anatomy of Dr Knox during the session of 1839 and 1840, but find no such person as John Henry Osborne of Epperstone.

Next Mr Fosbrooke obtained from Mrs Blagden, a doctor's widow of Long Clawson, Leicestershire, a certificate that Mr Osborne had been her late husband's assistant from 4 November 1843 to 2 November 1844, whereas he held the surgeons' certificate stating that he had "very regularly" been attending the surgical practice at the Royal Infirmary, Glasgow, from 1 November 1843 to 20 July 1845. This discrepancy Mr Fosbrooke was able to explain by contacting Mr Francis Sibery, a fellow student of Osborne's at the Infirmary, who had witnessed the actual signing of the document:

> I recollect standing in the lobby of the Glasgow Hospital towards the end of last summer session, which would be in July. Mr Osborne was there also, waiting for Doctors Lawrie and Hannay to fill up his schedule for the College of Surgeons. Dr Lawrie that day was late, and, as there were a number of students waiting, he took Osborne's schedule and signed it without filling up the blanks for the period he had been there, at the same time telling Osborne he could fill up the blanks himself. I also well recollect Osborne saying afterwards that he got Dr Lawrie's signature, and, to use his own words, "Now I can fill up my schedule for any length of time I like, as Dr Lawrie has given me his signature without filling it up." That was how the 21 months in Glasgow was obtained.

It was indeed a tangled tale, and as the *Lancet* observed, "if all the certificates were true, Osborne must have been acting three different parts at one and the same time," as his father's apprentice, as a school-boy at the Nottingham Grammar School, and as a pupil of Dr Knox at Edinburgh. It is interesting that in a second letter to Mr Fosbrooke, Mr Francis Sibery suggested that Osborne might have obtained Dr Knox's certificate from Mr Maddence, Knox's demonstrator: "I know they were great friends during the time he was in Glasgow. This is only supposition; but at any rate they are false certificates."

Naturally the publication of these facts in the *Lancet* led to a considerable correspondence on the subject in subsequent issues. More fuel was added to the fire by Mr J. S. Denham, M.R.C.S., who wrote that he had been a student at Glasgow during the years in question, and could prove without doubt that Osborne's certificate from Dr Lawrie and Dr Hannay for hospital practice was false:

> I do not wish to doubt Dr Lawrie's honesty; I believe him to be un-knowingly the instrument of a falsehood. He certifies to an attendance of 21 months, which is 18 months antecedent to his becoming surgeon to the hospital. In like manner Dr Hannay bears testimony to an antecedent period of 6 months. . . . That Osborne was not attending the Infirmary during the season 1843-44, I am well aware, as are others. He never was seen in the hospital that winter. . . . I will only add that Osborne told me, in Dr Buchanan's class-room, that his father pre-dated his indentures to enable him to obtain his examination at Apothecaries' Hall in accordance with the curriculum prior to 1835.

By this time Dr Hannay was dead, but Dr Lawrie wrote a letter to the *Lancet*, which was published on 26 June 1847. In it he said:

> Some months ago Mr Belfour [Secretary to the College of Surgeons of England] enclosed the copies of the certificates which Mr Osborne had procured for attendance on my lectures on surgery, and for hospital attendance in the Glasgow Royal Infirmary, and begged to be informed if they were correct. I replied that the certificate of attendance on my surgical lectures was correct, but that the hospital certificate was false, and had either been falsified or obtained on false pretences. To this letter I had no answer, and not having seen the schedule, I am not in a position to say which of these suppositions is correct.

Unfortunately Mr Belfour did sometimes fail to reply to his correspondents, and in this case it did look as though the Royal College of Surgeons of England was dragging its feet, and that the last thing it wanted to do was to take disciplinary action against the erring Mr Osborne. It is true that in the first place the Surgeons had been put into rather a quandary; the matter had

PLATE 7

William Hare.   A contemporary drawing by D. McNee.

From *Burke and Hare* by William Roughead, by courtesy of William Hodge and Company, Ltd.

come up in the spring of 1846, just before the vacation, and when they had asked the various signatories to verify their signatures on the certificates—which, incidentally, they all did—they had found that it was not possible to contact Dr Knox immediately, as he had gone abroad and they had to await his return. The attitude of the lecturers well suited the standstill policy of the College, as can be seen from the letter of its legal adviser, Mr Wilde, written in September 1846. This letter, which the *Lancet* dismissed as "full of doubts and quibbles, framed so as to check any idea of prosecution or punishment" ran as follows:

> I need not say that before any proceedings are adopted, there must be clear evidence of the untruth of the certificates, as it does not appear that there is any doubt of such certificates having been signed by the persons by whom they purport to be signed. The question as to the correctness of Dr Knox's certificates appears to be the most material; and the principal document disproving such certificate as to his (Osborne) being at Edinburgh from 4 November 1839–1st May 1840 appears to be the certificate of Mr Burder, the master of the school; that, however, you will perceive, only states that he left at Christmas 1839, as appears from the school register; and it is inferred that he, therefore, could not have been at Edinburgh from 4th November till Christmas. This I do not think sufficient, as his name might appear on the register, although he was not actually there. Some evidence should be furnished that he was at the school during that period, and also evidence that he was not at Edinburgh from Christmas 1839–1st May 1840. This, you will perceive, is indispensably necessary, as it appears that Dr Knox does maintain that his certificate is substantially correct.

In a leading article on 5 June the *Lancet* put the case fairly and squarely:

> Dr Knox says that Osborne commenced attending lectures on 4th November 1839, while Mr Fosbrooke states that he was only apprenticed "in the spring of the year 1840."
>
> We are minute about these certificates from Dr Knox because they really constitute the gravest part of this extraordinary case. If it can be shown that youths at school, before they have actually commenced their apprenticeship, can obtain certificates of attendance at lectures and that these certificates are allowed to pass unchallenged by the examination bodies, why then, there is an end at once of all security and fair play to the diligent student, the laboriously educated practitioner and the public; and diplomas and licences from the examining bodies must fall immeasurably in their value; they can, in fact, be no proof whatever of regular medical education and professional proficiency.

According to Mr Wilde, legal adviser to the College of Surgeons, Dr Knox admits that the certificate is actually signed by himself, so there is no suspicion of forgery on the part of Osborne. All the suspicion which attaches to this part of the case consequently lies at the door of Dr Knox.

As soon as Dr Knox had admitted the genuineness of his signature, the means of conviction in his case were obvious enough. The Rev. Mr Burder might have been appealed to; Mr Sculthorpe, whom Mr Fosbrooke maintains to have drawn up the real indenture; Dr Thompson, of Nottingham, with whom Osborne is asserted to have been living as assistant in 1840, might all have been called upon for evidence in a court of law, if need were, which would have shown plainly enough the truth or falsehood of Dr Knox's two certificates. Nay, the College of Surgeons ought to do so now, if they have any sincere desire to vindicate the honour of the members of the College. The suspicions of the case are sufficiently grave, and warranted by such evidence as to render this the bounden duty of the College.

But on 19 June 1847, the *Lancet* returned to the attack:

> Now that the facts are known no squeamishness ought to prevent parties who are desirous of upholding the respectability of the College and profession from acting in such a manner as to ensure justice. The party offending has merited the most severe punishment which the profession can award, and to suffer him to go unscathed is winking at fraud and forgery; it is holding out the reward of immunity to all others who have acted, or who may in future act, after the same manner.

Still the College made no move. It would have been easy enough, as the *Lancet* suggested, to condemn Osborne on the further testimony of Osborne's schoolmaster, of the lawyer who had drawn up his indentures in 1840, and of the doctor to whom he had been assistant in the same year, but nothing was done. Perhaps the Surgeons of England would rather help the rascally Osborne than Dr Knox. Osborne, at any rate, was allowed to retain his College of Surgeons' diploma.

The Court of Examiners of the Society of Apothecaries was even more pusillanimous. In the summer of 1846, after considering all the evidence laid before them by Mr Fosbrooke, it was decided that "no sufficient reason existed for refusing Mr Osborne an examination on the ground of fraud." On 6 August he was permitted to sit for his examination, and received a certificate of his qualification to practise as an apothecary.

The case of Mr John Henry Osborne, M.R.C.S.(Eng.), L.S.A., was to all intents and purposes now closed; he continued to practise and prosper at Epperstone, and lived happily ever after. Dr Lawrie, who like Knox, had signed an inaccurate certificate, was a graduate of Glasgow, and far from taking proceedings against him, the authorities there, two years later, appointed him Professor of Surgery in the University, and from 1858 until his death in the following year he represented the Universities of St. Andrews and Glasgow on the General Medical Council. But the Royal College of Surgeons of Edinburgh had not yet finished with Dr Knox.

On the 14 June 1847, Mr Scott, the Secretary of the Royal College of Surgeons of Edinburgh, wrote to Dr Knox to draw his attention to the *Lancet* of 29 May, with all its revelations about the Osborne case. In the circumstances he asked Knox, as he had apparently "authenticated" his signature, to say whether he had really granted the certificates or not. If he had, then the College expected proof that Osborne had indeed attended the courses, and proof which would "enable the College to rebut the evidence brought to prove that he was not, and could not have been in Edinburgh during the time specified."[68]

This was surely an example of most illogical reasoning. Mr Fosbrooke in the *Lancet* had proved that Osborne had falsified certificates recklessly, that in the vital year 1839-40 he was but a twelve-year-old schoolboy and it should have been clear to unprejudiced men of good will that Dr Knox had once again fallen victim to a rogue. It was, in fact, a rather strange case of history repeating itself, although this time murder was not included. But in the twenty years which had elapsed since the Burke and Hare case, Dr Knox seems to have learned nothing of the elements of self-preservation. Once again he thought—and after reading those pages in the *Lancet* one can hardly blame him—that no one could possibly imagine him to be the guilty party in this case, and that, as other surgeons had been as careless as he, the matter could be treated lightly.

Dr Knox was in London in June, and it is a pity that he did not keep silent as he did in 1828. He appears to have penned his

68 R.C.S. (Ed) Letter Book.

answer to the Edinburgh Surgeons in one of his more reckless moods. His letter, unforunately, cannot now be found; it is not preserved in the archives of the Royal College of Surgeons of Edinburgh, but the gist of it can be gained from Mr Scott's second letter to him, dated 29 June, in which he was asked to elucidate points in the reply which he had sent to the Secretary's previous enquiry of 14 June.

First of all there was the all important question of the signature. In this reply of his, undated but received in Edinburgh on 28 June, Dr Knox apparently declared the two certificates to be forgeries, both as regards contents and signatures—despite the fact that he was said to have admitted the latter to be genuine when interrogated by the College of Surgeons of England. The Secretary of the Royal College of Surgeons of Edinburgh, writing hurriedly to Mr Belfour in London, quoted the relevant passage in Knox's letter. Knox had written:

> Having examined the schedule of Mr Osborne presented by that gentleman to the secretary of the College of Surgeons of England and now in his hands, we, that is Mr Belfour and I, are quite satisfied that the signature of my name and the filling up of that part of the schedule having reference to the matter in hand are not in my handwriting.

Very rightly Mr Scott pointed out to Mr Belfour that:

> There must be something wrong here, and as you are named by Dr Knox as concurring with his opinion of the handwriting, and by Mr Fosbrooke as having given a very opposite account to him, I have to request that you will do me the favour to state whether you can afford any explanation calculated to remove this apparent contradiction.

Mr Belfour did reply to this on 7 July, and he wrote again in the last week of August, but both letters have disappeared.

If Dr Knox had had any sense of the seriousness of the situation in which he now found himself he would have stated simply that the certificates were forgeries, and left it at that. But, as can be seen from the further points in his letter which the Surgeons on 29 June asked him to "elucidate," he went out of his way gratuitously to produce damning evidence against himself, although he may have merely fancied that it was a good opportunity to expose what he had already called the "low, disgraceful, and entirely unprofessional" state of the educational establishments. Knox knew very well what was going on in the medical underworld, and in this lost but all important letter, quoted by Mr Scott, he stated that during twenty years three applications at least had been made to him to substitute a false date for a bona-fide attendance; he admitted that sometimes certificates had been signed by his assistant, with his authority, and that once or twice the assistant did not merely sign the certificate, but signed his name in his presence. Worse still, and Knox's candour is startling, the Secretary understood him to assert that:

> The transference of a date from one year to another, in order to make a certificate to suit the curriculum of some licensing body is "a very harmless matter," provided that the person "really did attend the lectures somewhere."

Here Knox was probably comparing Osborne, who had at least done a nine months' course, with those young gentlemen who had by even more contemptible means, procured forged certificates without attending any lectures at all.

Yet by giving expression to these ideas, Knox was indeed foolish beyond belief and was actually providing the rope for his own hanging. A letter of his, received by the College on 4 August, is mentioned, although it also has disappeared. As it was held to be "unsatisfactory," he cannot have spent much time on "elucidation." So, on 2 August, at a meeting of the President's Council of the Royal College of Surgeons of Edinburgh which considered the affair, it was decided that the whole correspondence with Dr Knox should be circulated to members, and the following resolution, proposed by Dr Gairdner and seconded by Mr Macfarlane, was passed:

> That the College having publicly announced many years ago that they will "withdraw their recognition" from any Lecturer who "evades the faithful enforcement" of the regulations, do now make known that Dr Knox has incurred that forfeiture by the certificates granted to Mr Osborne, and by the unsatisfactory character of his reply when he was called upon to justify them, and that no further Lectures delivered by that gentleman shall be received by this College as qualifying for their Diploma.[69]

---

[69] R.C.S. (Ed) Minutes, 2 Aug. 1847.

This, of course, was a dire penalty. It meant professional ruin. On 3 September, at a meeting of the College, Dr Gairdner moved and Professor Syme seconded a motion, which was carried unanimously,

> that the following letter be sent to Dr Knox:—
>
> Surgeons' Hall, Edinburgh.
3rd September 1847.
>
> "Sir,
>
> "At a meeting of the Royal College of Surgeons of Edinburgh held here this day, the whole correspondence which I have had with you was produced, and I am instructed to inform you that the College is fully resolved to disallow all future courses of instruction given by you, if they do not receive a satisfactory answer to my letter of 29th June last, on or before the 18th inst.
>
> "I am, Sir, etc.,
"(Signed) JOHN GILLESPIE,
for JOHN SCOTT, Secy., R.C.S.E."[70]

Dr Knox was not a man to be coerced by threats, and the 18 September passed without any reply from him. His sense of the utter injustice of the treatment accorded to him must have been intensified by the knowledge that, although in 1846 the College of Surgeons of England had allowed Osborne to go scot-free, they had, in this very year, on 29 April 1847, requested James Dore Blake, a pastry-cook of Taunton, to return the diploma granted to him because it had been acquired by "false statements" after only one year of alleged study, *i.e.*, a course three months longer than Osborne's. The *Lancet* provided an explanation of the difference in the action taken in the two cases:

> It was because in 1846 there was no immediate fear of a Registration Bill, and of a Parliamentary Committee of Inquiry; in 1847 the Council of the College of Surgeons have both these fears before their eyes; hence their galvanic attempts to appear as defenders of the profession, by the punishment of wrong-doers.

Be that as it may, what a difference it would have made to Knox if the cases had been reversed in time. He then might still have been free to lecture, with all his wealth of knowledge; while Osborne, with his minimal medical education, would never have been allowed to practise and to reach the heights

[70] R.C.S. (Ed) Minutes, 3 Sep. 1847.

he did: medical officer of the Calverton work-house, and surgeon to the Nottinghamshire House of Correction.

Meanwhile in Edinburgh the Surgeons seem to have had some doubts as to the legality of their proposed action. They went the length of taking Counsel's opinion, and on 16 October the reply of this gentleman, Mr John Marshall, Advocate, was put before a meeting of members in the form of three resolutions, drafted by Marshall, but moved by Dr Gairdner and seconded by Dr Maclagan:

> 1. That until Dr Knox shall give a satisfactory answer to the letter of the Secretary, R.C.S. (Ed) of the 29th June last, no certificate of attendance on lectures or instructions to be given by him after this date shall be received by the College as evidence of compliance with its regulations by any Candidate for its Diploma.
>
> 2. That a copy of these resolutions be immediately transmitted by the Secretary to Dr Knox's address.
>
> 3. That unless such an explanation as is referred to in the first resolution be received by the Secretary on or before 1st November next, these resolutions with the correspondence which has taken place on the subject with Dr Knox shall be intimated to all the Licensing Boards in the Kingdom.

These were carried with only one dissentient voice, that of Mr Alexander Hunter, and he alone, brave fellow, again dissented to the vote of thanks to Dr Gairdner "for his exertions in sifting the facts of this case, in putting the whole matter upon such a clear footing, and in bringing it to such a satisfactory conclusion."[71]

Dr Knox apparently did reply to this. His letter of 29 October was acknowledged by the Secretary who informed him that it would be laid before the College at the quarterly meeting on 12 November. The President, however, considered this letter, of which there is no copy, to be "a communication of rather a dubious nature,"[72] he discussed it with Mr Marshall and the result was that he reported to the meeting that "no satisfactory answer to the Secretary's letter of 29 June had been received from Dr Knox," and it was decided—Mr Alexander Hunter dissenting —that "the third resolution as submitted to the College at their meeting on 16th October be now carried into effect." The Secretary was therefore instructed to transmit copies of the whole

[71] R.C.S. (Ed) Minutes, 16 Oct. 1847.
[72] R.C.S. (Ed) Letter Book, 1 Nov. 1847.

correspondence and of the resolutions to all the Licensing Boards in the Kingdom.[73]

On 9 December 1847 Dr Knox received a brief note from the Secretary of the College:

Sir,

I send you a copy of Resolutions of the Royal College of Surgeons of Edinburgh, and of other documents, all of which you possess.

In compliance with the third resolution I have sent copies to all the Licensing Boards in the Kingdom.[74]

No less than twenty-two Licensing Boards were notified, and one of the more extraordinary things about this extraordinary case is that today not one of those still in existence can produce the correspondence. So Knox's letters in his own defence are for ever lost.

For a second time Dr Knox had been "hounded out of society." His wanderings now were destined to continue for close on a decade, his genius being continually frittered away. But Knox was resilient: in 1842 he had written "there is, according to some physiologists, a sixth sense, viz. the sense of resistance, by which we feel that we are not alone in the world."[75] Alone now, he would continue to fight on to the end.

15

Dr Knox's prospects at the dawn of the year 1848 were, to say the least, bleak. He toyed with the idea of going to America to deliver his *Races of Men* lectures, which were to be published in book form in 1850, but the scheme was abandoned. He revisited France, but was not impressed by the Paris of Louis Philippe. He went to the Jardin des Plantes and found Cuvier's skeletons

Mouldering and decayed. . . . In the Museum of Natural History fanaticism and prudery had been at work. The collection was in all respects neglected. The nude marble statue of Venus had been removed

[73] R.C.S. (Ed) Minutes, 12 Nov. 1847.
[74] R.C.S. (Ed) Letter Book, 9 Dec. 1847.
[75] *Lancet*, 11 Feb. 1843.

from the centre of the museum, and thrust into a low, damp, underground cellar-like apartment amongst the dolphins.[76]

Things were certainly not what they used to be. Of his masters in his student days, Cuvier, Geoffroy, and De Blainville, only De Blainville, the distinguished teacher of Comparative Physiology, was alive. He made a kindly attempt to help his old pupil by suggesting that Knox should now translate his works, as he had already translated his *Lectures*, but with "additional remarks and drawings." Knox did not follow up this suggestion, but he did use his knowledge of French to translate *Fau's Anatomy of the External Forms of Man, intended for the use of Artists, Painters and Sculptors*, and under this title the translation was published in 1849, with a preface added by Knox, and an appendix—running to about 100 pages—devoted mainly to criticism of the Elgin Marbles. At the time Dr Knox was living in London, off the Haymarket, and he had spent many of his hours of enforced leisure in the British Museum, studying these Greek sculptures with the keen eye of the artist and the anatomist. Surely no one but Knox would have drawn attention to the anatomical knowledge of the antique sculptor of the Theseus, who modelled the knee-cap so accurately that he showed not only the "crest of the tibia," but "the attachment of the ligament of the patella to the tuberosity of the tibia."[77]

This specialised knowledge certainly made Dr Knox an art critic with a difference. He points out, for instance, the beauty of the hands of the thirteen figures in Leonardo's "Last Supper"— "not a coarsely made vulgar hand"[78] among them—and he was led to consider the question of the greatest painters' knowledge of anatomy, and the use they made of it. For more than two years he cogitated over the problem of the true relationship of anatomy and art, and then in 1852 he published two books, one which he called a progressive school book, his *Manual of Artistic Anatomy*, the other the much more ambitious and successful *Great Artists and Great Anatomists*. The anatomists were, as might be expected, Cuvier and Geoffroy; the artists were Michael Angelo, Leonardo

[76] *Great Artists and Great Anatomists*, p. 80.
[77] *Fau's Anatomy of the External Forms of Man*, p. 220.
[78] *Great Artists and Great Anatomists*, p. 155.

da Vinci, and Raphael. Although Knox thought Raphael to be perhaps the greatest of the three, yet Leonardo may well have been for him the most interesting, since he believed that Leonardo alone had pursued anatomical studies without permitting them to "mislead him as an artist."[79] Michael Angelo had, he thought, allowed himself to be so misled:

> Whilst second to no man in power he was apt to give an excess of muscular force seldom displayed in the efforts of living man.[80]

Knox believed that this overemphasis was an error; the artist should conceal his knowledge of anatomy "as Nature has done, from the gaze of the world," keeping it in reserve to prove the correctness of his power of observing living forms. Leonardo had succeeded in this, and Knox quoted his *Sketch Book* to prove it. It is a tribute to Knox's methods of diligent research that he did not write his book until he had tracked down—and obtained permission to study—this *Sketch Book* in the Royal Library at Windsor, where it remained unpublished until 1938. Knox noted that in it Leonardo always drew:

> the living limb, with its glorious exterior, side by side with the dead and dissected corpse. He draws the dead as dead—the living as living. . . . The dissected muscle, besides being dead, is quite unlike the living in form, and in every other quality.[81]

Further study of the *Sketch Book* confirmed Knox's views on Leonardo:

> I have always thought that many, at least, of the anatomical drawings of Da Vinci,—and I am now certain of the fact, having examined for myself the sketch-book of the great Leonardo—were made by him merely to acquire an exact idea of the position of the various parts of the skeleton, and the extent of motion in the joints.[82]

Knox's criterion of great art was that it should reproduce the living form, and this is where he considered that Raphael excelled, although he had been no student of anatomy:

> Raphael's knowledge was derived from the study of living forms . . . his knowledge of form, of proportions, and his perception of truth were

[79] *Great Artists and Great Anatomists*, p. 136.
[80] *Op. cit.*, p. 148.
[81] *Op. cit.*, p. 161.
[82] *Manual of Artistic Anatomy*, London 1852.

absolutely perfect . . . of anatomy he knew nothing . . . after 300 years Raphael's portraits seem still alive.[83]

The antithesis of this Knox found at the Great Exhibition of 1851, where the statuary neither roused his sympathy, nor received his admiration, because of its total absence of a "life-like" surface. "The essentially Beautiful," Knox believed, "must be in Nature"; nevertheless the artist should not expose the anatomy of the human form, "that hideous machinery which nature intended should never be seen." Sculpture and painting should be "clothed with the bloom of eternal, ever-returning youth," for men have an innate dread of dissolution, and shrink from seeing signs of decay in the aged and infirm.

It is unlikely that Knox's reflections on art influenced many artists, but they made him aware of the two conflicting "cultures" of science and the arts, which are still unreconciled. He stated the position clearly, and was one of the first to do so:

> The gulf which separates the man of science from the man of letters, was not, and is scarcely yet understood.[84]

He himself, the anatomical and classical scholar, turned by necessity into a polymath, willing to speak and write on any subject, did as much perhaps as any man to bridge this gulf, and yet he remains for us very much the archetype of the modern scientist.

For Knox a love of science implied a love of truth, for him, "Mind was everything":

> The history of man is the history of his mind . . . great minds see truth, and truth only; they have no fancies; legends and miracles are out of their sphere. . . .[85]

> The grand qualities of the human mind . . . which distinguish man from the brute; a desire to know the unknown; a love of the perfect; an aiming at the universal . . . but to discover new and unobserved phenomena, and to detect new relations in phenomena already observed . . . that is genius.[86]

---

[83] *Great Artists and Great Anatomists*, pp. 188 and 195.
[84] *Op. cit.*, p. 66.
[85] *Races of Men*, p. 341 and 405.
[86] *Great Artists and Great Anatomists*, p. 21.

To observe new phenomena and new relations; this is what Knox would have wished to do. What he actually did in that same year of 1852 was to start writing a best-selling hand-book, a *Manual of Human Anatomy*, published in 1853, of which he seems to have been rather ashamed. To Professor John Goodsir (whom he considered his most distinguished pupil in anatomy) he presented an advance copy, rather pathetically explaining that, although he had always entertained a dislike of "Vade Mecums," he was "obliged to comply with the spirit of the age." Goodsir acknowledged the receipt of the book, spoke of the pleasure he had in reading it, and added:

> I have been astonished to find how much of what I have been in the habit of conceiving as peculiar to my own course of lectures I had derived long ago from you. I assure you I have always been deeply grateful to you as my teacher, and I have always, in public as well as in private, expressed myself to this effect, and shall not less continue to do so henceforward. I have strongly recommended your book to my pupils.

(There was something almost prophetic about this letter of Goodsir's. Over thirty years later he was so moved to wrath by R. L. Stevenson's "Body Snatcher," published in the *Pall Mall Gazette* "Christmas Extra" of 1884, that he took up his pen and sprang to the defence of his dead master:

> It will be said, of course, that the *Body Snatcher* is only a piece of fiction. A pleasant piece of fiction, certainly, to attach the stigma of cold-blooded deliberate murder to the name and memory of a man who has relatives and friends and admirers amongst the few still living of his many thousands of pupils.
>
> Was it out of delicate consideration for their feelings that Mr Stevenson made use of the K——, when he well knew that he might just as well have written KNOX.
>
> It would have lessened the flesh creeping effect of Mr Stevenson's sensational piece of fiction had he made himself acquainted with the true facts of the case. That the accusation against poor Dr Knox never amounted to more than mere vulgar *fama clamosa*. That the Crown Law Officers failed in eliciting one tittle of evidence upon which to found a case against him. That a Committee of leading Edinburgh citizens spared no pains for many days in weighing all the evidence, and in their Report entirely cleared and exonerated Knox from either knowledge of, or participation in, the Burke and Hare atrocities. . . .

When in the guise of fiction an author maligns in the most unmistake-
able terms the memories of men who have not long departed, he should
recollect that some one still may live who can answer and refute his
calumnies.)

The *Manual*, even if its author disapproved of it, got a good
press and sold well. The *Lancet* gave it an encouraging review,
calling it "without exaggeration a model book," one which every
student should possess.

It was not from choice during these years that Dr Knox lived
solely on his literary earnings. He applied for a Government
appointment for a survey in Africa, for which he was surely
practically, if not politically, a most suitable candidate. Despite
the fact that his candidature was supported by the Marquis of
Breadalbane and Sir George Sinclair, he was unsuccessful. It was
unlikely that those in authority would have forgotten his earlier
remarks about the Kaffir war.

Then, after spending so much time studying the Elgin Marbles,
Dr Knox took a logical step when he applied for a post which fell
vacant at the British Museum, but he did not get it. It can have
done him no good to have made comments such as these in a
note to his *Great Artists and Great Anatomists*:

> When Cuvier visited commercial England he discovered the only
> specimen of the cranium of the Balaena Mysticetus, the whale of com-
> merce, at that time in Europe, in a dark vaulted cellar below the British
> Museum; unheeded, unknown, and covered with soot and dust. Beside it
> lay the cranium of the South-sea whale. I found them many years after-
> wards in the same place. Zoological science could descend no lower.
> Matters are not improved.

A friend in Edinburgh told Knox to be careful how he spoke of
the management of the Museum, or of those holding office:

> You will make enemies who may do infinite mischief, and not the less
> because all you say against them is true.

But Knox was incorrigible. He, too, had been a museum curator,
and a very efficient one.

Then suddenly on 8 October 1853 an announcement appeared
in the *Lancet* which made it look as though Knox's years in the

wilderness were at last coming to an end. The statement ran as follows:

> Royal Free Medical College.
>
> We are requested to state that Dr Robert Knox has recovered from his indisposition, and will deliver his introductory lecture on Monday evening, 10th October at 7 o'clock.

In an adjacent column a reviewer expressed the hope that Dr Knox's *Manual of Human Anatomy* would prove "as successful as it is notorious that his oral teaching was, and is likely to be in the chair of Anatomy at the Royal Free Medical College."

The Royal Free Hospital was then twenty-five years old, and had been established for ten years in its present position in Gray's Inn Road. It owes its foundation to Dr William Marsden, who after finding a dying woman in the street, and failing to gain admission for her either to St. Bartholomew's Hospital or to Guy's, because she had no "letter" from a Governor, decided to build a "Free" hospital, where their sufferings alone would be sufficient recommendation for the sick poor.

William Marsden was a man of vision, who must have had much in common with Robert Knox, and who also suffered persecution when fighting for his hospital. He was three years younger than Knox, and, like him, had been one of Abernethy's pupils, so it was very natural that in 1853, when he was considering the establishment of a Royal Free Medical School, he should invite Dr Knox to lecture on Anatomy. In her book, *Surgeon Compassionate*, Frieda Sandwith, Marsden's great-granddaughter, writes:

> It was proposed that the three surgeons (Marsden, young Wakley and Grant) should rent the top floor of the building at the back of the hospital quadrangle, and two rooms on the ground floor . . . for the purpose of forming a school to be called the Royal Free Medical School. This proposal was made "with the full conviction that the committee of the hospital will, from time to time, use their best endeavours to extend the hospital accommodation so as to get it recognised by the Royal College of Surgeons, and with the understanding that immediately the hospital shall be recognised the school and the hospital shall be united."

In the *Lancet* of 13 August 1853, an announcement was made that "On 1 October a College in connection with the Royal Free

Hospital will be opened. The new buildings are progressing. There will be attached to the College a very extensive Museum."

A month later, among the Medical School Advertisements, appeared the syllabus for the autumn session of the Royal Free Hospital Medical and Surgical School. There were to be lectures in Anatomy and Physiology, Chemistry, Principles and Practice of Medicine, Surgery, Forensic Medicine and Materia Medica. The lectures in Descriptive and Surgical Anatomy would be given by Dr Robert Knox "daily at half-past nine. One session £5 5s., perpetual £8 8s."

This notice was followed on 4 October by Dr Tyler Smith's inaugural address for the Hospital's new session, in which he said:

> I have also undertaken the greater responsibility of introducing the Royal Free Hospital and its Medical College as a new organisation destined, we cannot doubt, to the teaching and cultivation of medical science through succeeding generations.

But, as is well known, the Royal Free Medical School did not open its doors until 1874. There are no records to explain why the scheme of 1853 failed when so near to fulfilment, but what happened then to Dr Robert Knox is only too clear.

It had been rash of Dr Knox to assume so readily that the Royal College of Surgeons of Edinburgh would forget the Osborne case and overlook his breaking of their ban. On 8 October 1853 —the very day on which Dr Knox's lecture was advertised in the *Lancet*—Dr Gairdner brought the matter before the College.[87] He reminded them of the events of 1847, when they had informed every Licensing Board in the Kingdom that they no longer recognised Robert Knox as a lecturer, yet here was Dr Knox advertised as a Lecturer in the Free Medical School of London. The Council was not prepared to stand any nonsense of that sort; a letter was at once despatched to the Royal College of Surgeons of England, asking if, in view of the correspondence of 1847, they did, or did not, recognise Dr Knox's lectures. The reply seemed eminently satisfactory: the Court of the London College had decided that it could not receive "certificates from Dr Knox

87 R.C.S. (Ed) Minutes, 8 Oct. 1853.

of attendance on Lectures delivered by him while the explanation demanded from him by the Royal College of Surgeons of Edinburgh in 1847 is withheld."

Even this was not enough for the Edinburgh Surgeons; they wrote again to ask if the Royal College of Surgeons of England had intimated their Resolution to the Lecturers of the Free School, "in order that the students attending it may be on their guard with respect to Dr Knox's lectures." To this they received a short answer: "as the said School has not been recognised by this College, the necessity of the communication referred to by you has not arisen."[88]

As far as the Royal College of Surgeons of England was concerned, the correspondence was closed, although it is very possible that it played some part in the delay in recognising the Royal Free Medical School, and might explain why Marsden proceeded no further with his scheme at that time.

A certain mystery surrounds Knox's advertised inaugural lecture. Lonsdale not only states that he gave it, but that:

> he was said to have made an impression upon his audience. He alluded to the circumstances which had borne down upon his Edinburgh career, and showed the gravity of the anatomists' position in England previous to the year 1830.

If this were really so, this lecture would be invaluable in any study of Robert Knox's life and work, but unfortunately, no record of it appears to exist. Indeed, in the circumstances, it is difficult to see how Dr Knox could legitimately have delivered it, and reasonable to wonder if, in fact, he ever did. There is no doubt that two immovable forces had met in head-on collision, and were equally unyielding: the Royal College of Surgeons of Edinburgh remained as obdurate, and Knox as stubborn, as in their previous encounter.

Knox never again attempted to defy the Royal College of Surgeons of Edinburgh, and until 1874, no more was heard of the Royal Free Medical School.

With Knox, personal tragedy always seemed to follow professional failure. As in 1841, so now: hardly had the vision of

[88] R.C.S. (Ed) Minutes, 16 Dec. 1853.

154

PLATE 8

Photograph of Sir William Fergusson, Bart., F.R.S., Serjeant-Surgeon to the Queen, and President of the Royal College of Surgeons of England. He was Knox's senior student at the time of the murders, and his life-long friend.

By courtesy of the Royal College of Surgeons of England.

the new Royal Free Medical School faded, than bad news came from Scotland. In May 1854, his son, Robert, a most promising young man, died suddenly in Edinburgh after a heart attack. It took months for Knox to recover from the shock, and it may be for this reason that his next book is so unlike all the others.

Unhappy in London at any time, he turned in his sorrow to his memories of home, and produced a little 1s. volume on *Fish and Fishing in the Lone Glens of Scotland*, which became an instant success. Fishing had always been Dr Knox's favourite recreation, and in the writing of this book, when he was lonely and miserable in the London he hated—"that monstrous assemblage of bricks and mortar, commonplace and sham," where he lived "pent-up, debarred from fresh air, exercise, and the contemplation of Nature's work"—he found a nostalgic pleasure in recalling those happy far-off days when, on his "good grey mare, Bess," he had crossed the Lammermuir and sought the rivers of southern Scotland which he described so well, Esk and Tweed, Yarrow, Ettrick, and Gala Water.

He relived the scene so completely that he gave detailed directions of the routes to be followed to particular beats, some-times over desolate moorland where the road was "difficult to find in thick weather, dangerous to take in snow." He warned his readers of other dangers which might beset them: the Solway bore, the quicksands of Dunbar, the treacherous pools of Tweed. He gave practical advice about clothes: a suit of Scottish plaiding he considered best, and wrapped up in a waterproof bag, hose and wading shoes. He advised "a stout salmon rod, reel and line from fifty to sixty feet," and for trout he suggested minnow as a bait, provided the angler was a man not less that 5 feet 10 inches in height, with a strong arm and hand, and able to make the minnow "spin or revolve dexterously, and to touch the waters as softly as a fly." Occasionally, like every fisherman, Knox would tell his own success story, as when fishing for sea-trout one day with a grilse fly, he landed a seven-pound salmon.

Knox had no intention of competing with the *Compleat Angler*. His book was the work of a scientist, indeed, in it he quoted all too frequently from his early papers on the food and dentition of the trout and salmon, but he had this to say of Izaak Walton:

> Happy contented Izaak! You were never troubled with the desire to discover the unknown in the past nor in the present, sufficient for you was the fact that it is so. . . . Nevertheless, it is pleasant to see what a refreshing book may be written by one devoid of genius to observe anything, but simply blessed with a love of nature sufficiently strong to narrate what he felt and saw.

In this context "observation" was, for Knox, a highly specialised and scientific faculty:

> To observe Nature, and to discover the absolute truth, requires, in many cases, more than good eyes and a brain: it requires knowledge or experience, previously-instructed sight, otherwise the object may be before you, and yet remain wholly unseen or unperceived by you.

Knox was neither happy nor contented, but he still had immense vigour, and motivated either by patriotism or professional zeal, or perhaps by both, his next aim was to reach the Crimean battle-field. In 1854 Knox was sixty-one years of age, but he put every iron into the fire to get himself sent out to the Crimea either as a physician or staff-surgeon. Lord Murray wrote to Lord Panmure from Edinburgh to recommend his application, and Knox also enlisted the aid of his old student, Fergusson, who wrote:

> You seem to me as full of energy as ever, and I need hardly say that your intellectual powers seem equal to any of those former efforts which in early days made you dux of the High School of Edinburgh, and the first teacher of anatomy in Europe.

Of himself, Knox wrote, "I am still the same as when you first saw me, full of life, mad after the discovery of the unknown in science."

It was all in vain; Dr Knox was not accepted by the Army Medical Department, though it might have been happier for those in authority if they had allowed him to become a regimental surgeon again. From London he bombarded the War Office and the Admiralty with suggestions for the better conduct of the war:

> He had correspondents in the Crimean Army, and was well posted on all movements of the besieging force [at Sebastopol]. He knew the hardships to which his professional brethren were exposed, the faulty commissariat, and all the evils of the situation; and used his pen pretty freely

to show up the errors of the Government in the *Morning Advertiser* and
other newspapers.

From this it might be assumed that the pages of the London press
were full of irate letters from Dr Knox. Inspection of the files
proves that this is not so; in the correspondence columns of the
Morning Advertiser there are no letters signed by Knox. It is,
however, possible that Knox was the "correspondent" of that
newspaper who rapped official knuckles in shrewd and Knox-like
style:

> One word more—stiff stocks and close-buttoned coats are not discarded
> in June on active service, after all that has happened. A new Albert hat
> is going out for the unfortunate men who have survived all other
> disasters.[89]

16

Dr Knox's story would be one of unmitigated tragedy had he not,
towards the end of his life, been able to return to the fringes, at
least, of his old world. The doors of the lecture-room were for
ever closed to him, but those of the laboratory and dissecting-
room remained open, and in 1856 he was offered the most suitable
post imaginable. On 23 September the Committee of the Cancer
Hospital, by a unanimous vote, appointed him pathological
anatomist to the hospital. He took up the position on 18 October,
and continued to do excellent work there—without any sort of
friction—until he was stricken by mortal illness.

The appointment must have made some amends to both
William Marsden and to Knox for his non-recognition as a
lecturer at the projected Royal Free Medical School three years
earlier. In 1851 the Cancer Hospital (Free), like the Royal Free
Hospital, had been founded by Dr Marsden, who early recognised
the need for a special hospital for cancer patients "where, from
the instant the patient is seen, he is carefully watched to the close
of the case." The hospital did not move to the building in the
Fulham Road until 1862, and in Knox's time its departments were
still widely spread over London, between the Waterloo Road,
West Brompton, and Piccadilly.

[89] *Morning Advertiser*, 15 Jun. 1855.

157

The work of pathological anatomist in such a pioneer hospital must, for Knox, have been very congenial. His hand can be traced at work in the hospital museum, where with "untiring industry" he arranged a collection of post-operative and post-mortem preparations. The writer of Dr Knox's obituary notice in the *Lancet* refers to this, and also to the great interest he took in the general welfare of the hospital.

Professor James Syme had been unable to prevent this appointment, but he had not yet finished with Knox. In a letter he sent to the *Lancet* in November 1856, commenting adversely on a description which William Fergusson had published of Liston's manner of holding the knife when performing lithotomy, he said acidly that Fergusson had never been a pupil of Liston's, owing to his intimate connexion with Dr Knox, "of whose dissecting-room he had the principal charge during a very eventful period." Fergusson was prepared to overlook slighting references to himself, but he had always been loyal to Knox, and the raking-up of the old Burke and Hare scandal, just at this particular moment when Knox had at last regained his professional status, was more than he could bear. He rushed into print in the correspondence columns of the *Lancet*; under the very suitable heading chosen by the sub-editor, "Audi alteram partem":

> Allusion has been made in Mr Syme's letter to my connexion in early life with Dr Knox. How such connexion could have in any way influenced either Mr Liston in the method in which he held his knife in lithotomy, or my appreciation of it, I cannot possibly comprehend. My impression is, that the allusion has been made for other and despicable motives. I have ever been proud to acknowledge my early association with that distinguished anatomist and teacher, and much of my success in life I gratefully attribute to the advantages I enjoyed as one of his assistants. I reckon it no small honour to have had what Mr Syme calls "the principal charge" of dissecting-rooms, wherein upwards of 200 pupils were educated annually for an "eventful period" of about seven years, during which time I was favoured with much of Dr Knox's professional confidence. That position gave me an influence and a start in life which few men between the age of 19 and 26 ever possessed, and it was from it chiefly that I could presume to enter as a teacher the field of surgery, already occupied by Turner, Liston, Lizars and Syme.

William Fergusson had always been Knox's favourite pupil; he watched his brilliant career with pride, and in London

Fergusson was one of the few of his old students with whom he remained on intimate terms. Sir Benjamin Ward Richardson, who also saw Knox occasionally at this period, has recorded how jealously the old man guarded his independence, how resolutely he was determined not to compromise his friends; how frankly and tragically he accepted his position in the eyes of the world:

> He would sit with me a long time, and then would leave "to have a chat with William"; but he spoke on no other subject than science, and never, under any pressure, however courteously invited, would taste a particle of refreshment. There would sometimes be a stranger or strangers in the drawing-room, but he never would be introduced into it. . . . Where Knox lived while he was in London I did not know.

Knox was, in fact, then living in Hackney. When the fires of social ambition had been quenched; when, as Richardson so well describes, he fled the fashionable society of London's West End, he found peace and content in the East. When the Cancer Hospital gave him the first permanent post he had held for over a decade, he ceased to be a wanderer and settled down to home life at 9 Lambe Terrace, Hackney, with his only surviving son, Edward. His devoted sister, Mary, who had followed him from Edinburgh, also lived in the district until her death in 1858.

In Hackney, where no one knew anything of the horrible past, Dr Knox built up a little practice, and called himself "the happiest of practitioners." He was kind to his poorer patients, charging them no fee, and often giving them food and luxuries, which he could ill afford. Money had little meaning for him when it was no longer convertible into "subjects" and "exhibits"; only a few weeks before his death he said to a friend, with all his youthful enthusiasm, "I would rather discover one fact in science than have a fortune bestowed on me."[90] But he must have been well aware by then that both the fact and the fortune had eluded him, and that time was no longer on his side; the years wasted in the wilderness had taken a heavy toll.

There is no doubt that Knox mellowed in his later years, and lost much of his bitterness as he passed into calmer waters; perhaps because he had begun to realise that he must come to

[90] *Lancet*, 3 Jan. 1863.

terms with death. In 1858 his eldest daughter, Mary, died at the early age of thirty-three, and in the words of her husband:

> The Doctor never got over the shock of her melancholy death, which seemed to have preyed very much on his mind and health. He expressed to Mr Renshaw, his publisher, at the time, that he then, and only then, saw that he was mortal.[91]

Knox retained his full mental powers to the end. He continued his journalism and published two more books, *Man, his structure and physiology*, and a translation from the French of H. Milne Edwards, *A Manual of Zoology*, a textbook which he hoped might do something to hasten the introduction of his "favourite pursuit," zoology, into the universities, "as a recognised branch of general education."

He continued also to study contemporary events, and gave them candid criticism. He read Darwin's *Origin of Species*, and dismissed it, saying, "it leaves the question precisely where it was left by Goethe, Oken, and Geoffroy Saint Hilaire." He followed closely the development of Africa, and regretted, as he believed Livingstone did, that the explorer had not shown his manuscripts to Dr Andrew Smith and himself to check the scientific statements. "As it was," he said, "Livingstone's book was unreadable, but it suited the Geographical and Missionary bodies."

In 1860 Knox had been made an Honorary Fellow of the Ethnological Society of London—the highest honour the Society could bestow—and honorary curator of its museum. It was at a meeting of the Society on 1 July 1862, that he spoke in public for the last time. The subject under discussion was a discovery of human bones, with special reference to a skull with "simian affinity," and the occasion was later recorded by one who was there:

> The present writer having spoken at great length on the subject, Dr Knox rose, and with a gesture of eloquence, entirely put right the whole matter, and corrected the errors into which both Mr Mackie and myself had been led. The manner in which the great old man then spoke will never be forgotten by those who heard him . . . the remembrance of the last occasion on which Knox spoke will be an eternal souvenir.[92]

---

[91] *Lancet*, 10 Jan. 1863.

[92] " Review of Lonsdale's ' Life ' by C. Carter Blake," *Journal of Anthropology*, 1870-1. I.

Only in that summer of 1862, in his sixty-ninth year, did Knox's strength begin to fail, and he recognised the symptoms of heart disease. The faithful Lonsdale was with him at the time, and he reports that Knox was

> fully aware of the approaching shadows of death; but this made no change in his conversation, and led to no religious manifestation.

Nor did he give up his work. On 9 December 1862, he attended the Cancer Hospital as usual, but came home tired and exhausted; during the night he had an apoplectic seizure, and died, almost without regaining consciousness, on 20 December.

Knox, a true countryman at heart, had asked to be buried at Brookwood, "where the sun might shine longest" on his grave, and where the wild flowers and heather reminded him of Scotland. His wishes were respected, and his grave can be found in the nonconformist portion of the cemetery, marked by a flat stone without inscription.

It would be difficult to find an epitaph for one so gifted and so thwarted, so persecuted and so misjudged. The medical journals brought out their obituaries, and concentrated on his kindness and generosity. The *Lancet* remembered his "most affectionate and cheerful disposition, his promptitude in doing any kind action which could serve another, his high intellectual qualities." The *Medical Times* made a few reservations, and singled out his "new speculations on philosophy . . . which may not agree with the notions of some Christians," also the bitterness with which he "inveighed against all authority, political, civil and religious." But in spite of this, and of the fact that "during a part of his career he was not free from all blemish," he was a man "pre-eminently tender, friendly, and affectionate . . . who inspired the greatest respect in all who were admitted to his friendship."

In this tragic life story of a great scientist, Edinburgh with her intolerance and jealousy, played a large part, and Edinburgh remained unrepentant to the end. The obituary notices of lesser men may be found in the pages of the *Edinburgh Medical Journal*, but it could spare no space to commemorate Robert Knox, a prophet without honour in his own country.

BIBLIOGRAPHY

I. MANUSCRIPTS

GOODSIR. Linked Memories, Fife Coast, etc. N.L.S. *c.* 1884. MS. 170.
KNOX, ROBERT. Letter of R.K. N.L.S. 1844. MS. 2618, f. 228.
Records of the Royal College of Surgeons of Edinburgh.

II. PERIODICALS

Caledonian Mercury, The.
Edinburgh Evening Courant, The.
Edinburgh Medical and Surgical Journal.
Edinburgh Weekly Chronicle, The.
Glasgow Medical Journal. c. 1923. "An Hitherto Unpublished Letter by Dr
 Robert Knox," [to Dr A. M. Adams].
Journal of Anthropology.
Lancet, The.
London Medical Gazette.
Medical Times and Gazette.
Morning Advertiser.
Scotsman.

III. OTHER PUBLICATIONS

BAILEY, J. B., ed. *Diary of a Resurrectionist.* London 1896.
BALL, JAMES MOORES. *The Sack 'em-up Men.* Edinburgh and London 1928.
BALLINGALL, GEORGE. *Life of John Barclay.* 1827.
BELL, SIR CHARLES. *Letters of Sir Charles Bell,* ed. Lady Bell. London 1870.
BRIDIE, JAMES. *The Anatomist.* London 1931.
CHRISTISON, SIR ROBERT. *Life of Sir Robert Christison,* ed. by one of his sons.
 Edinburgh and London 1885.
COCKBURN, HENRY. *Memorials of his Time.* Edinburgh 1872: first pub.
 Edinburgh 1856.
COMRIE, JOHN D. *History of Scottish Medicine to 1860.* London 1927: 2nd
 edn. 1932.
COOPER, BRANSBY. *Life of Sir Astley Cooper.* London 1843.
CORY, G. E. *The Rise of South Africa.* VOLS. I, II. London 1910.

CRESWELL, C. H. *Royal College of Surgeons of Edinburgh.* Edinburgh and London 1926.

CURRIE, A. S. "Robert Knox, Anatomist, Scientist and Martyr." *Proceedings of the Royal Society of Medicine.* (Sect. History) 1933. XXVI. 39.

Dictionary of National Biography.

Examination into the Causes of the Declining Reputation of the Medical Faculty in the University of Edinburgh. Edin. Burgess 1834.

GORDON-TAYLOR, SIR G. and E. W. WALLS. *Sir Charles Bell, his Life and Times.* Edinburgh 1958.

GRANT, ALEXANDER. *The Story of the University of Edinburgh.* London 1884.

GUTHRIE, DOUGLAS. *History of Medicine.* London 1945.

Hansard. 9 May 1829.

JOHNSTONE, COL. W. *Roll of Commissioned Officers in the Medical Service of the British Army 1727-1898.* 1917.

KNOX, ROBERT. *System Human Anatomy: on the basis of the "Traité d'anatomie descriptive" of M. H. Cloquet.* Ed. and tr. by R. K. Edinburgh 1829.

—— *Memoirs, chiefly Anatomical and Physiological read at various times to the Royal Society in Edinburgh.* 1837.

—— *Fau's Anatomy of the External Forms of Man, intended for the use of Artists, Painters and Sculptors.* Tr. with additions by R. K. London 1849.

—— *Races of Men.* London 1850.

—— *Great Artists and Great Anatomists: a Biographical and Philosophical Study.* London 1852.

—— *Manual of Artistic Anatomy for the use of Sculptors, Painters and Amateurs.* London 1852.

—— *Manual of Human Anatomy descriptive, general, and practical.* London 1853.

—— *Fish and Fishing in the Lone Glens of Scotland.* London and New York 1854.

—— *A Manual of Zoology,* by H. Milne Edwards. Tr. R. K. London 1855.

—— *Man, his Structure and Physiology.* London 1857.

LEIGHTON, ALEXANDER. *Court of Cacus.* Edinburgh 1861.

LONSDALE, HENRY. *A Sketch of the Life and Writings of Robert Knox, the Anatomist.* London 1870.

MACGREGOR, G. *The History of Burke and Hare.* Glasgow 1884.

MACNALTY, SIR ARTHUR. *Sir Benjamin Ward Richardson.* London 1950.

MILES, A. *The Edinburgh School of Surgery before Lister.* London 1918.

MOORE, NORMAN. *The History of St. Bartholomew's Hospital.* London 1918.

NORTH, CHRISTOPHER. See WILSON, JOHN.

Report from the Select Committee (H. of C.) on Anatomy.

RICHARDSON, SIR BENJAMIN WARD. *Vita Medica.* London 1897.

ROSS, JAMES A., and HUGH W. Y. TAYLOR. "Robert Knox's Catalogue," *Journal of the Hist. of Medicine and Allied Sciences.* X. NO. 3. 1955.

ROUGHEAD, WILLIAM. *The Trial of Burke and Hare,* "Notable British Trials Series." London and Edinburgh 1921.

SANDWITH, FRIEDA. *Surgeon Compassionate.* London 1960.

163

Scott, Sir Walter. *Journal*, ed. J. G. Tait. Edinburgh 1939.

Smith, Sydney. *Memoir and Letters of the Rev. Sydney Smith*. vol. i. London 1855.

Steven, William. *The History of the High School of Edinburgh*. Edinburgh 1849.

Stevenson, Robert L. "Body Snatcher," *Pall Mall Gazette*. "Christmas Extra" for 1884.

Stockenstrom, Sir Andries. *Autobiography of the Late Sir Andries Stockenstrom*. Cape Town 1887.

Struthers, Sir J. *Historical Sketch of the Edinburgh Anatomical School*. Edinburgh 1867.

Theal, George McCall. *Records of the Cape Colony*. vols. 12 and 13. London 1902, for the Government of the Cape Colony.

Thomas, Dylan. *The Doctor and the Devils*. London 1953.

Thomson, John. *Report of Observations made in the British Military Hospitals in Belgium after the Battle of Waterloo*. Edinburgh 1816.

Thornton, John L. *John Abernethy*. London 1953.

Turner, C. H. *The Inhumanists*. London 1932.

Wilson, John. *Noctes Ambrosianae*. Edinburgh 1829.